If Yes Is the Answer,
What Is the Question?

If Yes Is the Answer, What Is the Question?

George Kimmich Beach

Skinner House Books

Published by Skinner House Books, an imprint of the
Unitarian Universalist Association,
25 Beacon Street, Boston, MA 02108-2800.

Printed in the USA.

ISBN 1-55896-295-6

10 9 8 7 6 5 4 3 2 1
99 98 97 96 95

Acknowledgments

"Poem #822" by Emily Dickinson reprinted by permission of
the publishers and the Trustees of Amherst College from *The
Poems of Emily Dickinson*, Thomas H. Johnson, ed., Cam-
bridge, MA: The Belknap Press of Harvard University Press,
Copyright © 1951, 1955, 1979, 1983 by the President and
Fellows of Harvard College.

"The Fountain" by Denise Levertov is from *Poems, 1960-1967*,
Copyright © 1961 by Denise Levertov Goodman. Reprinted by
permission of New Directions Publishing Corp.

"Runes" by Howard Nemerov is from *New and Selected
Poems* (Chicago, IL: University of Chicago Press, 1963). Reprinted by permission of Margaret Nemerov.

"On Going Down in History" by Howard Nemerov. Copyright
© 1968 Christian Century Foundation. Reprinted by permission from the November 27, 1968 issue of *The Christian
Century*.

"Directive" by Robert Frost is from *The Poetry of Robert
Frost* edited by Edward Connery Lathem. Copyright © 1975
by Lesley Frost Ballentine. Copyright 1947 © 1969 by Henry
Holt and Co., Inc. Reprinted by permission of Henry Holt
and Co., Inc.

To Barbara Kres Beach

Contents

Preface

James Thurber once remarked that "it is better to know some of the questions than all of the answers."

In a world where religion is often associated with creeds and definitive answers, Unitarian Universalists tend to agree with Native American leader Ruby Plenty Chiefs: "Great evil has been done on earth by people who think they have all the answers."

Our congregations don't gather on the basis of the creedal question, "What do we all believe in common?" Instead, we ask covenantal questions: "In what spirit do we promise to walk together? With what hopes? What resources? What great questions?"

It matters what questions we ask. All good teachers know that. So do good ministers. And, as you will soon discover, the author of this volume, George Kimmich Beach—"Kim" to his congregants and friends—is both.

For one thing, he both knows our heritage and has been questioning it all his life. The late Rabbi Abraham Joshua Heschel often said that one reason why we don't understand our own religious heritage in the West is that we have forgotten which questions to ask. Instead of prophetic questions, like Micah's "What doth the Lord require?" (to do justly, love mercy, and walk humbly with thy God), we are such products of consumer society that our questions about religion are upside down: "What do *I* require? In a group, a cause, a teacher—a God that I'll trust?"

Not that these are bad questions, said Heschel. The prophets knew we must always choose between the greater and the lesser good. Our questions are bad only if we forget that, overall, something is asked of each of us.

Kim Beach doesn't forget.

This book is his way of helping a democratically oriented religion respond to Matthew Arnold's remark, "It is a very great thing to be able to think as you like, but, after all, an important question remains, *what* do you think?" (*Democracy*, 1861)

Or as philosopher G. E. Moore put it, in the preface to his *Principia Ethica* (1903), history's record of disagreement over ethical issues may be "due to a very simple cause: namely to the attempt to answer questions, without first discovering precisely *what* question it is which you desire to answer."

Our Chosen Faith: An Introduction to Unitarian Universalism (Beacon, 1989), which I wrote with F. Forrester Church, used ten story-based chapters organized around the five "sources" from which our free church tradition draws inspiration. Here Beach draws us one level deeper in understanding liberal religious commitment by organizing eight chapters around stories and questions of self-awareness, self-understanding, personal value judgment, and commitment to responsible action. He does not require that the reader respond in the same way that he does. Not at all. But his point of view, like that of a good questioner, is always there, to help sharpen your own.

Beach is a leading student and interpreter of the late James Luther Adams, widely acknowledged as the greatest Unitarian Universalist theologian and ethicist of this century. He collected, edited, and introduced two volumes of Adams's essays: *The Prophethood of All Believers* (Beacon Press,1986) and *An Examined Faith*, (Beacon,1991). Like his mentor, Beach always brings the free church and its members back to one basic question, "What are you using your spiritual freedom *for*?" Such questioning is grounded in a challenging and prophetic interpretation both of the Bible and of the liberal tradition itself.

Like the prophets, he is ultimately less tied up in sweeping metaphysical questions like "Why is there something rather than nothing?" or "Why is there such exquisite beauty—and such terrible pain?" than he is concerned with *practical* questions of religious living. His questions are directed to us: "How shall I express my affirmation of life? What means of nurturing my capacity for wonder and caring are meaningful for me? What values inform the choices I make? What commitments am I willing to make along life's way?"

In this, Beach reminds me that for many years I summarized the religious question as "What kind of story are we in?" This, of course, is a question that could only be answered if all six billion of us now on this planet were clearly characters in some great drama, much larger than any of our separate roles and perspectives could comprehend, and if the Author were willing to answer us directly. Instead, of course, I found myself searching the many classic stories, both scriptural and non-scriptural, for the Author's cues and clues. What I found, of course, is that those stories agree with Beach in re-directing us to what we should be asking, not of others, or of someone off-stage, but ultimately of ourselves.

Toni Morrison puts it this way in closing a story of human pain and questioning: "There is really nothing more to say—except why. But since why is difficult to handle, perhaps one must take refuge in how."

When it comes to the "how" of religious questioning and living, this volume offers help that is at once serious, insistent, and gentle—just like its author.

John A. Buehrens, President
Unitarian Universalist Association
January 1, 1995

Introduction

The most important word in our language is yes.
It matters what we say yes to.
It matters what we say no to.
Every no gets its value from the yes it also affirms.
To say no to what denies and destroys is also to say
   yes to what affirms, builds, creates.
God, said Nathan Söderblom, is the everlasting
   yes of existence.
>   Jacob Trapp, *Dawn to Dusk Meditations*[1]

Most of us know far more clearly what we do not believe than what we do. We may have strong opinions *about* religion, but when it comes to our personal convictions *of* religion, we are not so sure. Those who profess utter certainty about their beliefs often seem narrow and dogmatic; we find them unreliable and sometimes dangerous. Yeats, in "The Second Coming," lamented,

> The best lack all conviction, while the worst
> Are full of passionate intensity.

In face of the religious right today, we understand Yeats's lament. We do not want easy answers. We would rather take on the toughest questions of human existence and find pathways toward the discovery of our own answers. Still, we wish for a passionate intensity of our own. To such people—and here I include myself, for to write is also to discover—this book is addressed.

Beyond Pale Negations

The story has it that Gertrude Stein on her deathbed was asked, "Gertrude, what is the answer?" "The answer?" she replied, "What is the question?" We cannot rush into our spiritual void with affirmations, offering answers before we have discovered the questions. To find answers we must first rediscover the questions—the original questions of the religious quest.

"To say no to what denies and destroys is also to say yes to what affirms, builds, creates." (Jacob Trapp) Underlying and nerving our negations—our protests against "what denies and destroys"—are our affirmations, yet to be articulated. In the name of what, for the sake of what, do we protest? To ask this question is to begin to become conscious of our affirmations. The questions implied in our negations, then, are the questions to which we answer yes. The questions that we pose to ourselves in moments of existential decision give direction to our quest and shape its outcome.

I am not interested in answers that are half-truths dressed up as profundities, like the slogan, "To question is the answer," nor in clever riddles, like Zen koans that have been abstracted from Zen disciplines. Such ploys do not nourish my deepest need. I cannot offer them to nourish yours. Rather, I ask questions that help me find my own answers, thus enabling me to become more fully aware, reflective, purposeful, and effective.

To bring ultimate things to light is to begin to bring ourselves to light. Some questions enable us to progress, by stages, toward a more deeply felt and articulate faith. Bernard Lonergan has analyzed the conscious and in tentional operations of the mind, and on this basis outlined a sequence of four stages. Thus, to become more fully conscious and intentional is (1) to become self-aware, (2) to understand oneself, (3) to decide one's value-commitments, and (4) to act confidently and responsibly. These four stages in the movement toward heightened consciousness underlie the structure of this book.[2]

This quest has both personal and intellectual dimensions. They are equally important, and the book proceeds on both levels at once. To illustrate the dual nature of the inquiry, consider the question of God. The answer you or I give to the question of the meaning and reality of God will depend on what kind of a question we think it is. Is it a scientific question to be answered with empirical evidence? A psychological question to be answered in terms of personal need? A religious question to be answered by acceptance of God's self-revelation?

Theology touches on each of these perspectives, but two other perspectives seem to me central and decisive: "God" as a metaphysical question, to be answered by the logic of faith, and as an existential question, to be answered by a personal sense of ultimate meaning and moral concern. I believe that the best pathways are marked out by what I will call the logic of faith and by reflection on the meaning of human existence. The following comments will clarify what I mean by these two perspectives—the intellectual and the existential.

Paradox and Commitment

The medieval mystic Meister Eckhart said, "God is the denial of denials." The statement is intriguing at a purely intellectual level. The double negative reminds us of the algebraic rule: a negative times a negative equals a positive. Double negatives are supposed to be bad grammar, but we use them in two important ways: something "I *cannot not* do" is a moral imperative; something "I *cannot not* affirm" is a compelling belief. Paradox has been called "a bad sign of truth." Its intellectual cousin, the double negative, lies at the root of what I call double vision: the necessity of seeing the same thing in two different ways at the same time.

It is no wonder that we find it easier to say what we do not believe than what we do. Negation is the beginning of self-differentiation, just as the young child discovers "No!" as a way of asserting, "I have *my own* will." The wonder is that denial is a first and perhaps a necessary step toward affirmation. Jacob Trapp's rejection of pure negation points the way to a fundamental affirmation—an "everlasting Yes to existence."[3]

The quest for affirmations cannot bypass our mental and emotional negations, as "positive thinking" and "new age" thought typically try to do. Much religious talk boils down to the earnest but intellectually empty assertion that "it's good to be good."[4] Theology is, indeed, an intellectual exercise, and unless we are intrigued by its puzzles and attracted by its insights— if it is only a specious kind of poetry, or self-help psychology, or moral exhortation—we will finally be bored by it.

On the other hand, if statements like "God is the denial of denials" are only intellectual puzzles or academic "God-talk," our spiritual salt will have lost its savor and our theology, its existential bite. We will finally say, "That's interesting," and leave it at that.

An existential question is a question that touches one's very being, one's sense of identity or integrity; to answer it calls for a personal decision or commitment. Consider Eckhart's statement, "God is the denial of denials," in terms of your personal experience. The word "denial" recalls the despair, the cynicism, or the nihilism against which we struggle at the deepest levels of our being, most obviously in the face of death. Indeed, everyone must sooner or later confront the fact of mortality. We cannot block out significant realms of awareness and remain whole.

> This consciousness that is aware
> Of Neighbors and the Sun
> Will be the one aware of Death
> And that itself alone
>
> Is traversing the interval
> Experience between
> And most profound experiment
> Appointed unto Men—

Emily Dickinson's lines make me shudder; the poem concerns the soul's discovery of "its own identity" in "the interval" between birth and death.[5] Mere positive thinking will not do, for only in the total context of life does the spiritual wholeness we seek come into view.

So theology must be more than an intellectual game, a playing with theoretical possibilities without regard to what is experienced and deeply felt. It must touch our existence. It cannot bypass despair or other powerful and negative forms of consciousness. Neither can it become excessively inward and spiritual. "A purely spiritual religion," James Luther Adams has said, "is a purely spurious religion"—for we are physical, frail, and fallible beings who inescapably live and die in historical communities.[6] The idea of a "denial of denials" has an instant, intellectual appeal; it plays upon the imagination. But the struggle to deny the grip that denials have on our lives is an arduous labor and a courageous act, or it is a fake. The outcome is never certain. Our lives are "at risk."

Existential Self-Reflection

Our first questions, then, are at once intellectual and existential.

My use of the word "existential," although influenced by existentialism, does not invoke a particular philosophy; there are, after all, many "existentialisms."[7] Here it refers to a dimension of life that is so obvious it is often overlooked.

Young journalists learn to write objective news stories that answer the factual questions "what, who, when, where, how," and sometimes, "why." What we sometimes forget is that the story is also a personal report. Normally we assume that the writer is telling the truth, an unbiased and accurate reflection of what took place. But to check out our assumptions, sometimes we have to ask: "Did that *really* happen?" or even, "Did it happen at all?" Such questions do not ask for a description of the situation but for an existential or reflective decision about the situation's real existence.

We are asking for a personal judgment that can be answered yes or no. Thus, yes-or-no questions mark a decisive turning point in thought. They turn from what-who-when-where-how-why questions to questions of awareness, meaning, judgment, and decision. They turn from theoretical to existential questions. The latter cannot be answered apart from a personal reflection; they ask for commitment.[8]

Religion responds to our need for personal reflection. We ask the question of awareness: What excellence or beauty attracts my attention? We ask the question of understanding: What intelligible meaning does this reality hold? We ask the question of judgment: What values inform my decision about this reality—how do I evaluate it? We ask the question of responsibility: What commitments and actions follow from this awareness, understanding, and value judgment?

These four questions, variously worded, are threaded through the eight chapters of this book. Each chapter is headed by a yes-or-no question, to which my own answer is yes. The reader is invited to enter into a parallel process of reflection and decision. This may, of course, lead you to quite different conclusions from my own. But the value of the quest lies not in the destination but in the journey itself.

This is the only valid way I know of engaging in theological reflection—inviting you to travel with me as far as you will, comparing and contrasting your own experience and sense of meaning. The result is far from a closed system of answers, for each answer opens up further, more far-reaching questions. The aim, in Friedrich von Hügel's phrase, is "to grow in our very questions." It is to discover the basic issues of human life—the "first questions" that are rooted in our experience and that call forth our affirmations. Shakespeare, in *Hamlet*, famously devised "a play within the play." I am asking a question within the question: If yes is the answer, what is the question?

The Structure of the Quest

Bernard Lonergan's four stages of conscious intentionality, which I mentioned earlier, underlie the first four chapters of this book; taking them in reverse order, the second half of the book mirrors the first half. (George Tavard first called attention to this pattern in Lonergan's theological method.) The eight chapters of this book can be visualized as falling along a parabolic curve:

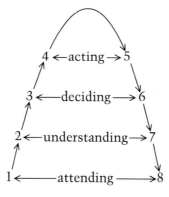

Not only are the themes of each chapter related successively, they are related laterally. There are internal relationships between the themes in chapters 1 and 8, 2 and 7, etc., on four levels of consciousness.

Read either successively or laterally, the odd and even numbers alternate. The odd-numbered chapters deal with what I have called the "inescapabilities" of human existence, while the even-numbered chapters deal with aspects of human freedom, suggesting another form of interrelationship among these themes: the transformation of life's inescapabilities is necessary for the fulfillment of our humanity. Thus, the book traces the following pattern of meaning.

The first and eighth chapters are concerned with religious awareness: the transformation of "the heart's directive," the longing for spiritual wholeness, by "parabolic vision," the capacity to see life as it really is and yet, also, with compassion, acceptance, and love.

The second and seventh chapters are concerned with understanding: the fulfillment of "the dedicated community" in its essential work—being the covenant people, the community of God—by uplifting and celebrating that which is sacred, by "naming God."

The third and sixth chapters are concerned with judgment and decision: the transformation of "the human condition," especially as it requires us to come to terms with tragic loss and evil, through a radical change of heart, mind, and will, which I have called "newmindedness."

Finally, the fourth and fifth chapters are concerned with responsible action in our personal and public lives: the fulfillment of "the moral covenant," the web of mutual caring that sustains our common life and rescues us again and again, through "creative freedom," the image of God in which we are continually made.

Reading the foregoing paragraphs is like consulting a road map before setting out on a journey. The map may be helpful, but the trip will not be much fun until you actually begin it and see where it carries you. May you enjoy the journey, and may you arrive at a new and better place!

1

The Heart's Directive

Are we incurably religious?

Don't say, don't say there is no water
to solace the dryness at our hearts.
I have seen

the fountain springing out of the rock wall
and you drinking there. And I too
before your eyes

found footholds and climbed
to drink the cool water.
                    Denise Levertov, "The Fountain"[1]

An interview with Thomas and Jean Sutherland on the
National Public Radio (NPR) news program, *All Things
Considered*, on December 10, 1991, caught my attention. Thomas Sutherland had just been released after
being held hostage in Lebanon for six and a half years.
He told about being chained, beaten, and isolated. Once
he tried to commit suicide. And yet he survived, appar-

ently unembittered and unbroken in spirit. How could he endure so much and emerge a whole person?

Sutherland spoke of his will to sustain whatever shreds of connection to others were still possible for him: the sometime companionship of other hostages, voices and music on a small radio during the later years, and, throughout the ordeal, the thought of his wife, Jean. She had traveled to Lebanon several times during his captivity, seeking his release. They learned by comparing notes after his release that on some occasions she had come close to where he was being held. Sutherland described having palpable feelings of her proximity during those times. When she left, he also felt the loss of her closeness.

It seems impossible to prove or disprove such reports of psychic communication; even if only imagined after the fact, they confirm the value of maintaining a sense of connection with loved ones.

Despite their physical separation, the Sutherlands managed to connect with each other, even though they didn't realize it at the time. Once, when Tom Sutherland and Terry Anderson were together, they requested a radio and the request had to go to the highest authority for approval. The following is a description of what happened, excerpted from NPR.

Thomas Sutherland: One of their intermediary types came in, by the name of Ali, and we asked him [for a radio]. And he said, "I have to take a *factoi.*" So he went and took a *factoi* in the—in the Koran. And he came back and said, "Oh, the news is bad."

Noah Adams: He wanted to do what?

TS: To take a *factoi.*

NA: Meaning?

TS: That's reading the Koran to see what the Koran says to a query. He did this query, and he decided the news was bad. And so I said, "How about another *factoi,* just for fun?" Later he came back and he said, "Well, I take another *factoi.* This time the news is good. You can have the radio."... And from that day until we went home, we had a radio.[2]

When Jean Sutherland learned about the radio from another hostage who had recently been released, she wrote to a BBC music program and asked them to play folk songs she knew Tom loved, songs also with an encouraging message, such as "Scotland, the Brave" and "Westering Home." Jean Sutherland said, "And I dedicated it to 'the best of men' and hoped that it would bring him home. And he did hear it. I couldn't believe that he did hear it!"

Connection and Compassion

Religion has been called "a sense of connectedness," and the Sutherlands' story makes that conception entirely concrete and human. Love, steadfastness, hope, courage—the virtues that they exemplified through their long ordeal—are spiritual "connectors" in human life. Nevertheless, the opposite seems to be the case with the only obviously "religious" person in the story, the young Muslim guard—a terrorist or an accomplice of terrorists, piously taking his *factoi*!

The guard does, however, show us something important about the nature of religion. He "takes a *factoi*" because an important and difficult question is at stake, and he fears making the wrong decision. He wants to know: What does Allah want me to do? Odd as the method may seem to us, it was his way of gaining confidence in the rightness of his decision. This too is what religion is: a way of gaining moral confidence by establishing personal connection to the highest authority.

Why, then, does the Muslim jailer take a second *factoi*, returning with the opposite answer? Apparently, he announced this answer not angrily but happily: "This time the news is good." Maybe the first inquiry was defectively executed, or maybe Allah changed his mind. But my guess is that Ali, the young warrior of Allah, thought: Is not Allah called "the merciful"? He seems to have felt a twinge of pity for Sutherland and

Anderson and sincerely wanted to do the right thing. The discernment of God's will, even for a Muslim fundamentalist, is not a science but an art—an art in which the deciding factor may lie in the inclination of ones own heart.

This too is what religion is: the inclination of the heart—an honest seeking, amid life's most difficult choices, of the heart's directive.

Discernment and Decision

The distinguished American poet Howard Nemerov said, "The poet's business is to name as accurately as possible a situation, but a situation which he himself is in. . . . The thought must be 'like a beast running in its skin' (Dante)."[3] What Nemerov says of poetry is also true of an authentic expression of religious awareness. It is not subjective fantasy but seeks, rather, to "name" spiritual realities "as accurately as possible." This naming or describing cannot be done from the viewpoint of an objective, external observer; the "situation" we discern and name is one we are *in*. It is an existential situation, addressed by existential questions—questions with present and personal import.

What, then, are the questions that shape our personal affirmations? If *yes* is the answer, what is the question?

The basic or "first" questions addressed in these chapters are not questions that ask for an objective description or, still less, for an explanation. They are questions of existence, questions that call for yes or no answers. I have deliberately framed questions to which my answer is yes. To be sure, you may answer no, at any point along the way, in effect refusing to follow the pathway I am suggesting. For instance, you may hesitate to follow Robert Frost's directive, in the poem called "Directive," namely to "lose" yourself on the vague promising of finding yourself:

> And if you're lost enough to find yourself
> By now, pull in your ladder road behind you
> And put up a sign CLOSED to all but me.
> Then make yourself at home. . . .[4]

Saying yes always involves an element of risk. You may hesitate to undertake the "ladder road" adventure to which he invites you, sensing that the place has an otherworldly atmosphere. "Directive" continues:

> The ledges show lines rules southeast northwest
> The chisel work of an enormous Glacier
> That braced his feet against the Arctic Pole.
> You must not mind a certain coolness from him
> Still said to haunt this side of Panther Mountain.

There is another possibility. Rather than yes or no, you could answer maybe. In which case I would reply: Why don't you take another *factoi*, just for fun? But whatever oracle or text you consult, be careful with your maybes. Tentativeness may be an intellectual virtue, but in the existential mode, as Hamlet discovered, it can spell tragedy. The only question that counts is the question you address to yourself: Can I find the spiritual wholeness I seek? Yes or no?

Auguste Sabatier, the French Protestant theologian of the last century, said that we humans are "incurably religious." If it is human nature to be devoted to ends beyond ourselves and to invest those ends with ultimacy, then yes, we are incurably religious. But make it a personal question: Am I incurably religious? You might say: "Well, yes, I am devoted to ends beyond myself—and that's very important to my sense of who I am. But I'm still not sure that it makes me 'religious.'"

The Presence of Transcendence

So let's look more closely at what being "religious" means. Rather than begin with creeds and churches, Bibles and Korans, Jimmy Swagart and the Pope, let us begin with ourselves, with the inclination of our own hearts. What do you respond to at the deepest level of your being with wonder, joy, hope, even with ecstasy?

One evening my wife, Barbara, and I went to the National Symphony concert without knowing what we were going to hear. (Truth to tell, we almost always go that way. It happens when you subscribe to a concert series months in advance and don't look up the program.) Reading the program on our arrival, I said to her, "It's an old war-horse, Grieg's piano concerto." I was ready to be bored.

On came the pianist, 20-year-old Peter Jablonski, and the silver-haired guest conductor Peter Maag, who could have been the soloist's grandfather. They began, they soared, and when it was over we cheered. There is no describing the thrill of the music, heightened by the sight of the pianist's absolutely authoritative hands and the graceful interplay between the youthful soloist and the aged conductor. It was the kind of ecstatic performance that draws you in, making you a participant in the event.

Remarkable aesthetic experiences are hard to distinguish from religious experiences, even though the art in question may have no specific religious content. In fact, few of us have difficulty with this idea, in an age when the art museum or the concert hall has become the temple at which many of us "worship." It may be more difficult for us to believe that, *even in church*, religious experiences can happen! For me it happened in a recent Sunday service while watching Betsy Fisher recreating Doris Humphrey's dance, "Two Ecstatic Themes: Circular Descent and Pointed Ascent" (1931). Ms. Fisher performed the rising, falling, ecstatic choreography with precision and grace, but to describe it seems impossible and pointless. The response that such a dance, conceived and performed with high artistry, evokes in us is at once physical and emotional.

But the meaning of the dance cannot be stated in terms of anything, such as a story or an idea, external to it.

The social context in which the artistic event takes place no doubt affects the intentions of the performer and the expectations of the audience, but that does not determine whether the dance or the music in question is "sacred" or "secular." The difference seems to lie in whether the performance calls forth an awareness of transcendence. By transcendence I mean the awareness of a fundamental condition of existence within which I find myself. I do not define transcendence; transcendence is that which defines me. Its recognitions are thus felt as "revelations." A creative event seems to take this form: *that* it is precedes knowing *what* it means. Perhaps we can say that the creative event reveals what Jonathan Edwards called "the beauty and excellency of being," naming his sense of the sacred reality that underlies and is manifested in all existence.

Again, I felt moved at the spiritual level of my being when the Reverend Donald Robinson preached to our congregation about his Beacon House ministry in northeast Washington, DC. Good preaching evokes our common faith and challenges us to new and enlarged commitment; just so, Robinson spoke both *for* us and *to* us. Here was a man of courage and sincerity, confronting the moral crisis of violence and the waste of young lives in our city; we were deeply moved by his witness and his selfless commitment. The beauty and excellence of a powerful social–ethical witness is very different from that of a performance or a painting; and yet, at some deeper level, it calls forth the same kind of response: we are in the presence of transcendence.

Is liberal religion too intellectual to "move" us spiritually? There was a time when Unitarians were tagged "God's frozen people." Reputations die hard, but I tell my people: Don't believe it. Believe in our music, our dance, our moral concern and courage. Believe in the inclination of your hearts.

Defining Religion from Within

To be sure, questions such as, What do you mean by "religion"? are important intellectual issues. But better than any definition is the experience of singing a deeply affecting song without taking exception to the words. A spiritual song is one that seems to come from somewhere beyond our conscious thought and invites us, irresistibly, to join in. Rather than carry the tune, we let the tune carry us. "Amazing Grace," for example, is a song that seems to have a life of its own; we could even say "it sings to us," giving voice to the directive of our hearts, when we give ourselves wholly to it. The directive points the way from restlessness to rest, from fragmentation to wholeness, from being lost to being found.

To take offense at the words to "Amazing Grace"— especially the phrase, "that saved a wretch like me"— may signify a fear of letting go of pain or guilt, lest the freedom we discover overwhelm us. Or, it may simply mean we are too "serious," when what we need is to be less literal-minded about religious ideas and more playful with our own feelings. In a Doug Marlette "Kudzu" cartoon, the Reverend Will B. Dunn is singing from his pulpit: "Amazing grace, how sweet the sound, . . . that saved a *stunted self-concept* like me. . . . I once was *stressed out* but now am *empowered* . . .was *visually challenged*, but now I see." In the last box he muses to himself: "Actually I never felt the lyrics to 'Amazing Grace' needed updating!"

An ability to laugh at ourselves is a sign of spiritual health, for it enables us to transcend ourselves.

Religion can be defined in highly elaborate terms, but the most insightful definitions are likely to be brief. The eccentric and beloved Harvard professor Arthur Darby Nock used to recite his elaborate and yet succinct definition: "Religion is what men [and women] in community do, say, and think, in that order, with respect to those things, real or imagined, over which they have no control." It is not an idealistic but a realistic definition, each term of which is worth contemplating.

We might wish to quarrel with Nock's focus on "things . . . over which we have no control," since it seems to imply human helplessness; in fact, religion is a way of acknowledging, coping with, and overcoming our helplessness. Just so, in his lectures on primitive religion Nock interpreted the religious mind as saying:

"The God who made the earthquake also made the incantation to avert the earthquake." This perception led to his short definition: "Religion is the refusal to accept helplessness." Lest we overspiritualize our understanding of religion—as if it were primarily a "feeling"—we should recognize that religion is centrally concerned with governance, on the cosmic, the social, and the personal levels. The religious person asks: What are the governing powers of the world, in harmony with which we should govern ourselves? The question of "control" comes back, but in a new form, as the question of self-control and self-direction.

Other short definitions illuminate other perspectives on the virtually universal phenomenon of religion. "Religion is ultimate commitment." (Henry Nelson Wieman) "My religion is my answer to the question I am." (Paul Tillich) "Religion is humility before the universe." (Anonymous) Any of these definitions could be elaborated into a dissertation; but consider another short definition, one that I find especially helpful: religion is our sense of "connectedness." The connectedness is both "intimate" and "ultimate," in James Luther Adams's terms[5]; it is both near and far, close and distant, personal and cosmic.

Symbolizing Religious Awareness

Richard R. Niebuhr points out that "religion," from the Latin, *religiare*, contains a metaphor: ligature, a connecting bond. Thus he offers the definition: "Religion is a kind of ligature by which we bind ourselves to divinity or that which bestows wholeness, by which we seek to bridge the distance that separates us from what is supreme in worth, calling forth our fidelity."[6]

It does so, Niebuhr says, primarily by symbols: "The ladder our aspiration climbs is not of ideas alone but ideas sheathed and growing within sensible symbols." Symbols are images suffused with feeling: a bridge, as in "Bridge Over Troubled Waters"; a ferryboat, as in "The Water Is Wide"; or a ladder, as in Jacob's ladder or Frost's "ladder road." Such images are "ligatures by which we bind ourselves to that which bestows wholeness." The sense of "bestowal" arises because the ultimate good we seek is given to us as a gift, estranged or "wretched" though we may be. It is a grace or charisma we enjoy, for no reason we can explain.

Although metaphorical, Neibuhr's words remain somewhat abstract. To illustrate his meaning he quotes an entry in the journal of the artist Paul Klee.

There are two mountains on which all is bright and clear: the mountain of the animals and the mountain of the gods. But between them lies the shadowy valley of humankind. When we gaze upwards—we who know that we do not know—we are seized, as in a premonition, with a restless longing toward those which do not know that they do not know and those which know that they know.

Klee's language, like his art, plays with symbols: the animals and the gods, two mountains and the shadowed valley between. In a few words he creates the whole landscape of the human spirit: one mountain inhabited by the gods, "who know that they know," the other by the animals, "who do not know that they do not know." We humans dwell between them, in a shadowy realm of uncertainty. We are aware of our separation from these other beings, and we long for their real or imagined blessedness. We humans know with certainty only that "we do not know," for we know that we are not gods. Thus we become "questions to ourselves." Still, we do know that much, and it troubles us in ways unknown to either "the animals" or "the gods."[7]

In philosophical terms, Klee's "animals" and "gods" represent the two limiting conditions that define our humanity, expressed by the paradox of "knowing that we do not know." But such abstractly expressed ideas omit something important that Klee's parable includes, namely the observation that we are forever dissatisfied with our limitations and seek ways to transcend them. Religion seems to be rooted precisely in the quest to transcend our normal limits, up to and including mortality. St. Augustine evokes this awareness in his *Confessions*: "And restless is our heart until it find its rest in Thee."

Animals, like young children, seem to dwell in what Paul Tillich called "dreaming innocence." We long for what we imagine to be the spiritual omniscience and freedom of the gods, and the moral innocence and unawareness of the animals. "We are seized, as in a premonition, with a restless longing"—toward what seems inaccessible to us, a realm of life beyond uncertainty and beyond fear. Where Paul Klee speaks of restless longing, I have spoken of the heart's directive. Religion is such an inclination of the heart—a longing, a directive—toward wholeness.

Journey, Guide, and Destination

The journey or the pilgrimage has long been a central image of the religious quest. To accomplish it we need a guide, a guru, a spiritual director. "Directive" has been an important word to me ever since I read and puzzled through Robert Frost's poem in Thomas Wittaker's English literature class at Oberlin College. The poem is written in the voice of a narrator who is also a guide, leading us on a pilgrimage up Panther Mountain in New Hampshire. The mountain is said to be haunted; so too is the destination, a place where human dwellings once had been but are no more. The guide leads us to

> . . . a house that is no more a house,
> Upon a farm that is no more a farm,
> And in a town that is no more a town.

All have been long abandoned. The locale is haunted, or

perhaps hallowed, by families, in fact, by an entire town and its culture. The people who once lived there are unknown to us, but we feel a kinship to them. Although long dead, they are not entirely gone. But don't be afraid, the guide says; if you have courage enough for the journey, these spirits can bless you. The mountain is sacred.

And who is "the guide . . . who only has at heart your getting lost"? Perhaps it is the natural inclination of the pilgrim's own heart, but it is experienced as "other," a voice that bids us surrender to its directives. The recognition of our need for a spiritual guide arises together with the sense of the strangeness, the "otherness," of "this place," as Jacob felt, after dreaming of an angelic visitation at Bethel (see Genesis 28). The guide says, "Then make yourself at home," nevertheless—here, amid the pathos of human labor and hope. We see first "the children's house of make-believe," and then "a house in earnest," the family home of which all that remains is

> . . . a belilaced cellar hole,
> Now slowly closing like a dent in dough.

Such is the setting of our spiritual quest, suffused with nostalgia for something pure and simple that has been lost. Although the object of our longing is obscure—we cannot define it but can only evoke it in parabolic language—we seek to recover it, nevertheless.

Sweating from the arduous climb, we seek refreshment. Instinct leads us to the farmhouse spring; we knew it must be there.

> Your destination and your destiny's
> A brook that was the water of the house,
> Cold as a spring as yet so near its source,
> Too lofty and original to rage.

Water is an ancient symbol of that which refreshes and renews our souls. It is the object of the spiritual journey evoked by the poem. Frost—or his guide—concludes:

> Here are your waters and your watering place.
> Drink and be whole again beyond confusion.

Seek the pure, original source of your being; follow the directive of your heart. The apparent conclusion of the spiritual journey is in fact its beginning.

Multifaceted Religious Experience

None of the several short definitions of religion cited earlier in this chapter tell the whole story, but each holds an insight into the nature of religion. Thus, when Thomas Sutherland asked his captor for a radio and would not surrender to despair, he showed himself to be an authentically religious person: religion is the refusal to accept helplessness. Why did the pious Muslim "take a *factoi*"? He was seeking Allah's directive; to him, the Koran is the source, his culture's central symbol, of "that which bestows wholeness." And why did he take a second *factoi*? Because, it seems, his conscience suggested to him that his first reading may have been wrong; it did not accord with the directive of his heart. Religion is also humility before "the universe," a reverence for life in its intimate and ultimate dimensions.

Apparently, the young Muslim was distressed by Sutherland's situation and unhappy with his own initial denial of the request for a radio, itself an instrument of sustaining "connectedness." The guard believed, surely, that the life-and-death struggle in which he was engaged had a spiritual import, and as such, he concluded that its aim could not be reached by denying utterly the humanity of the captive: it had already been grievously violated. Perhaps, in the sight of Allah, his own soul was at risk. The captor and the captive were connected after all.

The story carries a clue that, in fact, even this hardbitten warrior felt better when he was able to give a revised decision. At least, this is how I interpret his second response to Sutherland's request for a radio: "I have good news. The answer is *yes*!"

2

Naming God

Does the question of God presuppose God?

In the tablet of the universe, there is no letter
save Thy name. By what name, then, shall we
invoke Thee?

Jami, Muslim of fifteenth-century Persia

The power which is holy is also fragile. We are
constituted by it; it is sustained by us. . . . We who
are feminist theologians find much that is divine—work for justice, love, creativity itself, the
web of life, joy, and beauty. . . . We affirm that
these aspects of human existence are worthy of
worship. Attentiveness to the web of life, to the
exuberance of children, to the beauty of nature,
provides a sense of peace, of belonging, of exalta-
tion and ecstasy.

Sharon D. Welch[1]

When J. S. Bach concluded his last work, "The Art of the

Fugue," with music on the tones B-A-C-H, was it only a clever tour de force? Or was it his way of saying: My signature names a divine gift, an unaccountable genius for music I have been given? Consider the analogy: letters are to names, as names are to invisible realities, such as music, love, or human genius.[2]

Ancient wisdom read the letters (characters) of an alphabet as signs that reveal what is otherwise hidden from view—such as a person's character, something that is gradually told in the course of time. If the person's moral propensities were unknown or in question before an important assignment it would be especially important to discern in advance clues to the person's character. In Shakespeare's *Measure for Measure*, the Duke of Vienna so considers Angelo, his deputy who will rule the city in his absence, and addresses him:

> Angelo,
> There is a kind of character in thy life
> That to th' observer doth thy history
> Fully unfold.

Angelo's character, his moral quality, is revealed by his actions within the unfolding story. Shakespeare sometimes gives his characters names that suggest that they are not only individuals but are also "types," or symbolic figures. Young Miranda, for example, is full of wonder ("O brave new world . . . !") and Angelo is one who turns out to be a great deal "lower than the angels."[3] The capacity to name things is the capacity to discern otherwise hidden realities.

Letters and Names

I am interested in the act of naming as a clue to the persistence of God in the human heart and mind. Naming (or on a more abstract level, conceptualizing) is a fundamental aspect of human creativity; our "native tongue" is a living thing, a language we not only use but also create. Things become part of our usable world when we name them, or conceptualize them; yet, paradoxically, once we have named them, we have given them a life of their own, an independent reality that we cannot wholly "use" for our own purposes. I speak of "naming God" to point to this elusive, astonishing process by which we give distinct reality to the sacred and creative element in our experience. It is a God-like power and, at once, humbling.

The letters of my father, Stephen Beach, seem different in kind; they are epistles that serve as an Information Central for our whole extended, and sometimes distended, family. They knit us together. Many of their strands are drawn from the larger world beyond home and family, with running commentaries on the travail of liberal politics, the enjoyment of cultural and ecclesiastical events, and the glories of the passing seasons. I think my father likes the almost-lost art of letter-writing better than the long distance telephone call. It is not because he's old-fashioned; he is, after all, a diehard Democrat and a persistent supporter of the ACLU, the Southern Poverty Law Center, and many other progressive causes. Also, he is a Unitarian of humanist persuasion.

For several years I have saved a letter my father wrote to me one June, intending to respond to a comment he made on religion. His letter noted my then-impending journey to El Salvador: "I presume to further your education. One would hardly go there for another reason." The letter continued with reports on the perambulations of granddaughters and the grave illness of a son-in-law. It kept us up-to-date on the yard: "Our lawn and shrubs never looked better—in fact, they are perfect (or at least that for the amateur who takes care of them.)" To his backyard heaven, he made invidious comparison to a distant purgatory (a Unitarian does not believe in hell): "I can't imagine anyone preferring to live in California, with its crowds and fires."

His letters are a different sort than Jami, the Sufi mystic, had in mind, and yet they do bear his signature throughout—naming of those things that are of significance, and perhaps of ultimate significance, to him. Thus he inscribes the tablet of his universe. So do we all. Signing off, he said, "I guess that's all. The attached clipping goes with my humanism." It was a brief quote from the renowned cellist, Pablo Casals: "In music, in the sea, in a flower, in a leaf, in an act of kindness—I see what people call God in all these things."

Humanism and Theism

My father and I have carried on a debate over humanism and theism for a long time; but it is mild-mannered, neither of us really expecting to convert the other. It bemuses him, I think, that I doggedly stick to the theistic side. In the quote from Casals he found a theology in miniature. Nor will I call a "humanist theology" an oxymoron. Everyone reflects, at one time or another, on that which gives life meaning and value. In this sense, with or without God-language, everyone is a theologian.

The odd thing is this. Of the sentence that he said, "This goes with my humanism," I could have said, "This goes with my theism." Can we have it both ways? Suppose Casals had altered the order of his words and said, "I call *God* what people see in all these things." He would be saying: "Naming these things I name bearers of a mysterious, creative power. I am naming God."

Either way, Casals is giving a personal witness; he is exhorting us to see what he sees, to see beyond appearances. Obviously he does not mean that it is music, the sea, a leaf, a flower, or an act of kindness *in themselves* that people call God. He is pointing to *that in them* which makes them sources of wonder, or makes them expressions of what Paul Tillich called "the power of being," or Jonathan Edwards called "the beauty and excellency of being." He is saying: I call God that which I see in each of these things individually—or in all of them together.

The commonsense skeptic in us is likely to reply at this point: It's a nice sentiment, but why call it God? What people call God has meant so many things—some quite fantastic! Why not just take wonderful things as wonderful and leave it at that? Are there not also many terrible things in this world that could as easily be named? What about them?

Questions arise, on the one hand, around the pious tendency to ascribe all good things to God, when naturalistic explanations would suffice, and on the other hand, around the problem of theodicy: If God is just, why do the wicked prosper and the good suffer? When we raise the question of God, the questions tumble forth, because our minds anticipate a host of intellectual and moral issues. We do this, I think, because faith seems to promise a complete and consistent vision of existence. The logic of theology invites such a comprehensive vision, but never quite lives up to its billing. Too much does not fit the picture that has been painted for us; we may have felt cheated by our childhood faith. In the face of beliefs that have far-reaching and perhaps unforeseen implications, then, we guard our independence with mental reservations and objections. But rather than rush to answer all questions, we need to pause long enough to consider the directive of our hearts (what motivates our quest?) and observe the workings of our thought processes (what enables genuine understanding?).

Believing and Doubting

Taking one question at a time, we may ask again: Why not just appreciate wonderful things and leave it at that? Why drag in the God-question? I do so because, if our hearts are to reconcile the wonderful things that happen with the terrible things that also happen, it seems inevitable. I do so because the God-question is the central nerve of faith—the supposition that all things are reconcilable, or at least that there is a point at which heart and mind can say, "All manner of thing shall be well" (T.S. Eliot "Little Gidding," iii). Cut that nerve—declare the God-question settled and done with, or meaningless and irrelevant—and you cut the nerve of religious inquiry and concern.

There is, indeed, not only the wonderful in our experience; there is also the terrible. Always, we fall short of complete physical, moral, and spiritual well-being; we are less than whole persons in a less than whole world, and it troubles us. This recognition moves us from the theoretical to the existential mode; our sense of moral as well as of intellectual integrity resists easy answers and simple certainties. Much that passes for faith and much that passes for doubt appall us, for authentic faith and serious doubt come alive together.

Without questioning there can be no answering, and without doubting there can be no believing. No urge to name the sacred would arise were we perfectly omniscient, like the gods in Paul Klee's parable, or were we perfectly oblivious, like his animals. Either way, we would raise no questions and harbor no doubts. Neither the animals, who "do not know that they do not know," nor the gods, who "know that they know," are religious.[4]

It is precisely those who have a healthy sense of their own humanity—those who question, doubt, and believe without knowing—who are authentically religious. Paradoxically: *I question, therefore I believe.* It is those who imagine themselves almost gods in their wisdom, and those who behave like animals in their absence of self-reflection, who trouble and endanger us. Those who claim to be "above the law" regularly end up far beneath it, an illustration of Nicholas of Cusa's principle of "the coincidence of opposites." David Koresh, the self-proclaimed "messiah" who led his followers to self-destruction, is a graphic example. Authentically religious are those who, precisely because they know that they are free, recognize their need, in Richard Niebuhr's phrase, "to bind themselves to divinity, that which bestows wholeness." Naming God is such a way of binding oneself.

The Principle of Humility

The first questions of the religious quest are, as I have said, yes-or-no questions. They do not ask for information but for a decision. In the first chapter I asked, "Are we incurably religious?" and answered, "Yes, for knowing that we do not know, our hearts are incurably restless." We are at sea and seek our true north. If we have said Yes, we are incurably religious, then we must ask, Where is the resting-point within in this restlessness of the heart? For me, God is the symbol of that place.

The question I am asking in this second chapter, Does the question of God presuppose God?, may seem purely intellectual, but it too has an existential undertone. The question may be restated: Does the quest for transcendent meaning—something my life depends on in the face of apparent meaninglessness—presuppose the reality of transcendence? I answer yes, because I believe that the mind's unremitting drive to understand implies that there is something to be understood, although it eludes my full grasp. The recognition of that which transcends my finite understanding guards against self-validating fanaticism. My understandings are *partial* both in the sense of being incomplete and in the sense of being biased. The idea of God establishes the principle of humility: "I may be mistaken."

Emerson said we are riders forever falling off one side of the horse or the other. The principle of humility,

properly understood, does not lead to utter self-abnega-
tion, nor to a universal skepticism. Underlying the
"no" of no-claim-to-being-always-right is a "yes," a
positive, confidence-lending principle. I do not believe,
with Macbeth, that

> Life's but a waking shadow, a poor player
> That struts and frets his hour upon the stage
> And then is heard no more. It is a tale
> Told by an idiot, full of sound and fury,
> Signifying nothing.[5]

Shakespeare's very capacity to put our darkest dreams
into great poetry signifies the human capacity to transform and transcend them. No, I cannot make sense of
everything; that is why I depend on faith. Yet this is not
"blind faith" or faith that flies in the face of all evidence.
Life does yield some of its secrets to creative imagination and disciplined thought. As for the part that remains baffling and unintelligible to me, I strive to
"make sense" of it precisely on the assumption that,
ultimately, it is intelligible.[6] Otherwise, I would abandon these first questions and the religious quest itself.

"Proofs" of God's Existence

Logicians may object: Having an idea of something, for
instance a unicorn, the ancient Greek gods, or a man
named Macbeth, does not imply the existence of some-

thing. However, fictional animals or gods or persons stand for *something* in our imagination and become part of the world we experience and share with others. Some things are not *things* in the sense of objects of sense perception; they are nevertheless real. The denial that this is so marks the bewitchment of our intelligence by scientism, the belief that scientific objectivity is the standard by which all knowledge is to be measured. Rather, we are describing the way in which the human mind works—in particular, by naming realities that bear significance for us.

Questions about the validity of this line of thought persist. We want to ask: Why puzzle over theology, over naming God, when beautiful or wonderful things have perfectly good names all by themselves? Why this quest for Something Else behind everything that simply and plainly is? Many people do seem to function quite well on a matter-of-fact basis. To me, however, "everything" is far from simple or plain; things are not always what they appear; many things are baffling or wonderful; and much of what is most important to us depends on nonobjective forms of perception, such as imagination, insight, and intuition.

When we talk about God as an intellectual question, we may think first of the classical "proofs" of the existence of God. Take, for example, the classical argument from design: the world shows order and design, therefore, there must have been an Original Orderer, a Master Designer, God.

The difficulty is that the argument assumes that we know what we are looking for even before we start. The argument does not prove the existence of a supreme being called God; it presupposes an idea of God we already had in our minds. Such "proofs" are less than they seem; they do not provide rational proof of God's existence. (Paul Tillich went so far as to say it is improper to speak of the existence of God, since this makes God into a finite being in a world of finite beings, removing God's ultimacy.) In another sense the proofs of God are more than they seem, for they tell us something important about how the human mind works. Once again, the perplexing philosophical issue returns: What is the connection between the way our minds work and ultimate reality?

Faith As an Original Decision

Consider the logic of religion. Faith is not a well-reasoned conclusion but an original decision. It is born of the heart's inclination and the mind's orientation toward transcendence. God is not something that reasonable people conclude from arguments or evidence, but something that enables us to be reasonable by enabling us to recognize the partiality of our wisdom and to trust our mental and emotional instincts. God either enables me to make sense out of life, or God is nonsense—perhaps, as psychologists would say, a "crazy-making" idea. How odd! We set out to find

God, the ultimate, and end up puzzling over the intimate workings of our own hearts and minds.

A classic theological principle, articulated by St. Anselm of Canterbury (ca. 1033 to 1109 CE), expresses this insight into the workings of the human mind: "I believe in order that I may understand" (*credo ut intelligam*). This insight leads to the definition: Theology is faith seeking understanding.[7] Not the other way around: Understanding does not seek faith, for understanding is sufficient unto itself.

Some will say that's just the trouble with theology, it presupposes its own answer. Yes, but can you live purely by evidence or proof? Without "the surmise of faith"? Original decisions, suppositions on which you stake your life, are humanly inevitable. The question is, what original decisions enable understanding to grow? The question takes many forms, such as: What suppositions are trustworthy? How will you name that which is worthy of your devotion, that is, your God? A religious liberal is one who knows that, in principle, this question cannot be answered once and for all. James Luther Adams suggests:

> There are two quite different ways in which one may discuss theology. One may start with a definition of God, say as the Creator of the world, and they try to prove that [such a God] exists. . . . On the other hand, one may identify known realities or tendencies that are worthy of loyalty or that we

can rely on, realities that are ultimately a gift to us, realities that are viewed as sacred and sovereign, realities inescapable if life is to have meaning. If we speak of a reality as ultimately reliable, as dependable, as sovereign, as sacred, we are speaking of the divine whether we use the word "God" or not, and every human being . . . holds something to be dependable, something to be sacred, something to be sovereign.[8]

Here Adams invites us to name realities that we experience as dependable, sacred, and reliable. His favorite adjective is "reliable," and his favorite noun is "power." Sometimes he names God "reliable power."

Two questions—one religious, one ethical—follow: When and where do we find the power that is reliable in our lives? And what is our part in sustaining this reality? The religious question is directly linked to the ethical. Being a religious social ethicist (and an ethically committed person), Adams sometimes names God "the community-forming power." That power is ultimately reliable which creates a just and loving community among persons.

Religious liberals have been accused of preaching an excessively optimistic view of life. The charge is not entirely unfounded. The excess of optimism shows up in the liberal's tendency to assume that everyone is fairly healthy-minded (or at least curable) and in the liberal's incapacity to recognize and deal with human self-defeat and self-deception. Positive thinking is not enough because it discounts the negativities that are part of every person's experience. Taking the God-question seriously goes hand in hand with taking moral and spiritual failure seriously. Questioning God, struggling with the question of whether life "makes sense," often arises from the struggle to overcome one's own anger, grief, or despair. It is spiritually important, then, to recognize that beneath seemingly overwhelming negative feelings lies a positive motive, a longing for confidence and peace.

Does my struggle arise from the inclination of my own heart toward wholeness? I must answer for myself, yes or no.

Naming God/Naming Oneself

When one names that which is sacred, there is no abstracting oneself from the equation; you are saying, this is sacred to me. When Pablo Casals says "I see what people call God in these things," he is urging us to see them in this light also, and to name them sacred signs, letters of the divine name that cannot be fully spelled out. As much as he is telling us who he believes God is, he is telling who he himself is, or would be. Casals' religious vision, like Adams's, is a personally affirmed moral vision of the world.

In another wonderful sentence—this one was inscribed for me by my mother many years ago—Pablo

Casals said: "You must cherish one another. You must work—we all must work—to make this world worthy of its children."

People often ask, is your God a "personal" God? In the sense that God certainly is not a human being, a person, the answer is no. But more profoundly considered, I am impelled to say yes. A God who is impersonal will finally become subpersonal, something less than worthy of our ultimate concern as human beings, as persons.[9] The God we seek and give our devotion to must include our most personal concerns, like cherishing one another and working to make this world worthy of its children. God is that which enables the personalization of life.[10]

The lines between our search for God and our search for self are intimately intertwined. We cannot untangle them. I do not absolutely know who I am any more than I know who God is; as soon as I say, "I am this" or "I am that," I have set myself at a distance, as if I could examine the matter objectively. But the effort is ludicrous, for I do so from a hopelessly unobjective position.[11] What use is there of such a self-report? Maybe I'm trying to deceive you; maybe I'm deceiving myself. If I merely say, "Here I am," I am giving little information about myself, except what is spiritually most important, an existential commitment. I am saying: I am present, ready to respond, aware that I am I, a responsible self.

In the third chapter of Exodus, when Moses turns

aside to see the burning bush in the wilderness of Midian, a voice calls out to him, "Moses, Moses." He answers, "Here am I." Only now, being present and alive—not lost in nostalgia or longing—is he ready to respond to God's directive. And when he asks for God's calling card ("Who shall I say sent me?"), he receives the most mysterious answer of all: "I AM WHO I AM. . . . Say this to the people . . . 'I AM has sent me to you.'"

That the burning bush is "unconsumed" indicates that we are to understand this as a miraculous apparition, not a literal fire; we are not to confuse the name with the thing it symbolizes. Tradition names the voice from the bush "God," but it never says "God" is literally God's name. The story keeps God's name hidden, using only the mysterious formula "I AM WHO I AM." It suggests God's absolute freedom to be what God will; this "God" is the "original decision" from which all "reasons" follow. Biblical tradition warns against using the name of God in vain, thinking we can invoke the ultimate power and, like sorcerers, press it into our service.[12]

And yet, there is "the still, small voice" that addresses us, that asks us to be present, alive to the creative power that is present to us. There is that in us, not of our own making, that calls us, as Moses was called, to the labors of liberation. I call it creative freedom.

Reticence Transformed

I do not speak easily of God. It feels presumptuous, unless I retreat into a language of high abstraction and speak, as theologians endlessly do, about *the idea* of God. But intellectualizing wears thin. A meaningful discussion of "the God-question" drives us to speak in personal or existential terms. If religion, as the scholar of personal religious development James Fowler has said, is "the symbolization of our personal experience," God will be the symbol of symbols. That is, "God" will be the symbol of the drive to make sense out of life by symbolizing life in personal terms.

This entire chapter has been, perhaps for deeply personal reasons, a response to my father's letter. It is time to conclude.

You see, Dad, it's precisely the theist in me that moves me to speak of God with circumlocutions, such as, "Thou, the life of all our lives." It's a way of naming without presuming to define. And the humanist in me reminds me that, when I do so, I'm also naming and committing *myself*.

But we should not get so serious about all this that we forget to be playful. Call God "X," the unknown in the algebra of life. Life's equation cannot be solved: there is one unknown too many in the equation. There is also a "Y" term, myself. So I must take a stab at both at once, naming God by being personally answerable for my deeds and the character to which they bear witness.

More briefly, I name God by answering to my own name—by responding, Here am I!

To answer yes to the question of God, a question wrestled with at the deepest levels of my being, presupposes God. The argument has a logic of its own, perplexing and circular though it may be: I believe in order that I may understand; I seek that which enables me to make sense out of life; I name that which is "the denial of denials." And still I must ask: "In the tablet of the universe there is no letter save Thy name; by what name, then, shall we invoke Thee?"

I will answer: By the name that calls forth in me the creative possibilities of life: the power of being and the courage to be what I am, and more than I have been.

3

The Human Condition

*Can we acknowledge evil and
tragedy, and not lose heart?*

That there should be much goodness in the world,
Much kindness and intelligence, candor and charm,
And that it all goes down in the dust after a while:
This is a subject for the steadiest meditations
Of the heart and mind, as for the tears
That clarify the eye toward charity.
　　　Howard Nemerov, "On Going Down in History"[1]

Recently I got one of those telephone calls that regularly
come at suppertime from salespersons, charities, and
Democrats. When I picked up the phone and realized it
was an appeal for money, my first thought was: I wish
I'd let the answering machine handle it! Then the caller
said she was seeking support for MADD, Mothers
Against Drunk Driving. "Yes," I said, "I'll support that."
I find it difficult to turn down appeals for good causes,
but I had a special reason for saying yes to this one.

One night, a few years ago, the news reached us that our neighbors' 20-year-old son had been killed in an accident. Inevitably, my wife Barbara and I thought of our two sons, and reflected on how devastated we would be had such a thing happened to one of them. We walked over to our neighbor's house, but slowly, reluctantly.

To be faced with the painful emotions of a family in shock and grief is terribly uncomfortable. We could easily lose the courage and confidence that we need to do what we must do. Then we compare our fortune to theirs and wince at the difference. We empathize. We recall the Golden Rule. We go.

> To choose what is difficult all one's days,
> That is faith. Joseph, praise![2]

We do not have to do anything simply because we *can* do it. But in life, as in mathematics, two negatives make a positive: there are some things we cannot not do.

It was as bad as we expected. No, worse. The young man was returning home with friends after a concert and had stopped like the Good Samaritan to help the driver of a disabled car. A drunk driver in a passing car struck him. Mercifully, according to the report, he had died almost instantly. As our neighbors, husband and wife, in agony, told the story of their son's death, a second reason for their suffering became evident: How, they asked, could God have let this happen? If

God is a God of love, why our son? They are devout Roman Catholics. They consoled themselves with the thought that God must have had some reason, beyond our reasoning, for "taking" their son, some heavenly purpose for him to serve. *Some* reason, *some* purpose! The stark injustice of the event evoked unanswerable questions, and underneath, a crisis of faith.

The Spiritual Challenge of Tragic Events

Such questions about the meaning and justice of human existence drive us to ask about God. It is touching to witness a childlike trust that God will take care of "His own" and keep evil from our doors. But when tragic loss is suffered, we fear for the believer more than we would for the hardened cynic, for tragedy leaves the believer terribly vulnerable to a loss of faith. As a counselor I sometimes hear people who have met personal tragedy say "God let me down" and give this as the explanation for their sudden loss of religious belief.

But tragic events can also be a turning point in our lives. "I set before thee this day good and evil, life and death; therefore, choose life, that you and your descendants may live." (Deuteronomy 30 : 19) In our normal, everyday moods, choosing life seems easy and obvious: doesn't everyone naturally do so? In the face of tragedy and evil, the choice is burdened with difficulty. Why do people choose "death"—self-destructive paths? There are, of course, many reasons; the first step is to break through the veil of self-deception and acknowledge the behavior for what it is. People with self-destructive behaviors of long standing are likely to draw family members and friends into complicity with the denial of reality, so this can be especially difficult. Death is not simply a physical fact. As psychology since Freud has helped us recognize, it is also a spiritual reality— a possessive, "demonic" power, something with a life of its own.

"Life" and "death" are, then, symbols. When we "choose life," difficult as it may be for us, we are acting out of faith, tacit or explicit. Then the power of "death" to determine the direction of our lives has been broken. (Or broken in principle; perseverance is still required to effect a break with a life determined by death.) Once this spiritual conversion has been experienced, spiritual growth becomes possible. A more adult faith and a deeper moral commitment and caring become possible.

Being subject to tragic events is a fundamental condition of human existence. Recognizing our vulnerability is a fundamental condition of maturity. Recognizing tragedy and vulnerability, and not being embittered or driven crazy in consequence, is either heroic or a sign of grace. It seems inexplicable. When we witness it in others, we can only wonder at their capacity for self-transcendence; when we experience it ourselves, we are strengthened and we rejoice.

Responsibility and Compassion

Sometimes tragic events are accidental, hence apparently absurd, the products of blind chance. Sometimes, however, what we call chance events are compounded with irresponsibility—either somebody else's or, most difficult to acknowledge, our own. For instance, when alcohol is mixed with driving, "accidents" are no accident. And sometimes chance events—being "in the wrong place at the wrong time"—are compounded with intentional malice or apparent insanity; then evil becomes a stark reality. Sometimes a guilty conscience for our own irresponsibility or malice further complicates our feelings. But even if we are the victims of apparently chance events, we tend to imagine an independent agent behind them. Thus, young children may imagine that if their parents divorce, they are being punished for something that *they* have done. They need to be told that the divorce is not their fault, and told in such a way that they can actually hear it.

As adults we imagine that we have outgrown this childish logic, but in a crisis we often discover that we have not. Something bad happens, and we blame either ourselves or the Agent of agents, God. Sometimes we blame God even though we have said we do not believe in God. Tragedy is a no-win situation. Evil is a downhill slope. Tragedy and evil have a momentum of their own, and they are very hard to reverse.

How, then, can we acknowledge tragedy and evil,

and not lose heart, that is, not be overtaken by bitterness, or self-hatred, or despair? We cannot, unless we make of them occasions to deepen our recognition of the human condition and discover the healing power of compassion. Neither we nor others are exempted from the human condition, although its blessings and curses befall us unequally. Compassion embraces other beings, ourselves, and sometimes even God. It enlarges us by enlarging our world to include those who suffer and, unlike the priest and the Levite in the parable of the Good Samaritan, do not "pass by on the other side."

How shall we describe the human condition? As tragic? Yes, but not at all times and in all places. Our garden-variety sufferings are often exaggerated and are often self-inflicted. Then we are laughable and, with grace, can parody ourselves; laughter can heal. Is our condition then also comic? Again, the answer is yes. Both conditions, the subjects of classic drama, challenge us to grow. Sometimes life knocks us down and forces us to start all over again; sometimes the falling down is funny, as if executed by Charlie Chaplin. Sometimes it is a slapstick comedy, and sometimes, a horrifying tragedy. Pain and laughter are close kin.

Self-Appropriation

Religion deals with human intentionality, the directive of our hearts, minds, and wills. I have been asking and answering, chapter by chapter, a series of interrelated questions for self-reflection. Bernard Lonergan persuasively argues that these questions arise from a fundamental pattern within the conscious and intentional operations of the human mind. By reflecting on these mental operations, we heighten our self-awareness and our purposefulness—in Lonergan's phrase, our "conscious intentionality." The object is self-appropriation, that is, taking possession of our full intellectual, moral, and spiritual capacities.

Lonergan's analysis structures what would otherwise be a bewildering variety of religious questions. He outlines a scries of four, interrelated questions. First: What attracts my attention, concern, or wonder? Because I also want to understand my experience, I ask, second: How can I make sense of—conceptualize and integrate—this experience? Nor is it enough simply to understand, but on the basis of my awareness and understanding I must evaluate and choose. I go on to ask, third: What decisions of meaning and value do I make? Fourth and finally, I ask: In the light of this awareness, understanding, and decision, what commitments to act responsibly will guide and shape my life?

These questions, asked in various ways, form a cumulative series through which we heighten our consciousness of the human condition and become more fully intentional in our living. We do so, Lonergan suggests, when we operate under the guidance of certain overarching commitments of the mind. Lonergan calls them transcendental imperatives, namely: Be attentive, be intelligent, be reasonable, be responsible. Sometimes he adds a fifth imperative, transcending even these: Be in love.[3] I am inviting you, the reader, to draw on your own thought and experience, making this reflective exercise your own path to self-appropriation.[4]

When in the first chapter I asked, Are we incurably religious? I answered yes, because the human heart is necessarily given to something beyond itself. Then let us be attentive to the inclination of our hearts—toward the beauty and excellence of being.

In the second chapter I asked, Does the question of God presuppose God? I answered yes, because the quest for ultimate meaning supposes that there is an ultimate meaning to be found. Then let us have the courage of our questioning minds, now consenting to, now dissenting from, the world as we find it. "Naming God" signifies what Jonathan Edwards, the eighteenth-century American theologian, elegantly called "cordial consent to being."

A third question, asked in this chapter, builds on those preceding it: Can we acknowledge the most disheartening aspects of the human condition and still live confident, affirmative lives? The question is existential, and shows the contrast between a theoretical question—a question about human nature or about people in general—and an existential question—a question addressed to ourselves, about our existence. Questions that can be answered yes or no are existential questions; they do not ask for information but for a judgment. They are personal questions in the sense that someone must make a decision and then take responsibility for it. They are addressed not only *to* me but also ask *about* my sincere intent; for instance, "John, do you take Mary to be your wedded wife?" or God's question to the prophet Isaiah, "Whom shall I send, and who will go for us?" (Isaiah 6 : 8)

Being in Time and History

Our whole lives are shaped by the answer we give to such existential questions; they are both religious and moral. Cautiously intellectual preaching tends to stay on the theoretical level. Existential preaching, such as we hear in African-American congregations, moves from the level of exposition and storytelling to the level of application, where the preacher "convicts" the listeners; the congregation senses the difference, and *this* is when the responses come, "Amen!" and "Tell it, brother!" We are not simply asking whether people in general can bear up under the burdens of tragedy or evil; we are asking: Can *I* acknowledge evil and tragedy *in my own experience* and not lose heart?

"To be or not to be—that is the question."[5] Hamlet asked the original existential question. Hamlet dramatizes the vertigo of freedom that we feel when we recognize that we can decide what we will, and no one will tell us what our decision should be. Hamlet's tragedy turns on his repeated deciding not to decide, his incapacity to exercise his freedom. Existentialism asserts *that* we are before we know *what* we are. Until or unless we decide "to be," that is, decide *that* we are, we will not be able to discover *what* we are, because that will only be found in our actions.

Reflection on the human condition often takes on a melancholy tone. The reason may be that we discover who we are only after we have launched ourselves into life, and then it may be too late to do anything about it. In his lectures Paul Tillich was fond of quoting Hegel: "History is not the place of human happiness." The past has a fateful import; we carry the burdens of past actions with us and cannot easily free ourselves from them to begin anew.

To ask about the human condition, then, is to ask about our being-in-time. It is to ask about human life folded into history. History is the story of the birth, the life, the death, and (sometimes) the resurrection of human communities. The future is contingent; it depends on something we willingly choose before we entirely know what it means. On the Gettysburg battlefield Abraham Lincoln called for "a new birth of freedom"—a symbol of national resurrection—and the nation is still trying to discover what that new birth must be.

Lincoln addressed the human condition in his time and place, invoking its inescapability: "We cannot escape history." He has been called "America's greatest theologian," although the designation would have amused him, for he never joined a church.[6] Lincoln reflected deeply on the destiny of "we the people of the United States of America," because he had a profound sense of the human aspirations it represented and of his own place in history.[7] The issue of slavery was inescapable, he saw, because slavery contradicted the founding charter of the nation, which announced a universal human equality. And yet he knew that confronting the contradiction would bring on warfare's vast agony of death and destruction. The nation's wounds would be deepened before they could be healed. In the face of these limits, he asked, what possibilities lie before the nation, and what choices are open to me?

It is our fate to contemplate the possibilities and limits inherent in the human condition, as it presents itself in our personal and historical situation.

Human Nature and the Human Condition

Questions of evil and tragedy elude rational explanation. Shakespeare mused on "the evil men do," acts that are both freely chosen and destructive; yet freedom itself eludes explanation. Thus, "the capacity for self-determination" may come close to defining human nature, and yet the concept is paradoxical since it defines "the human essence" in terms of an idea of indeterminacy. Conversely, tragedy—evil which befalls us due to circumstances utterly beyond our control—

seems to cancel human freedom; and yet, a "tragic vision" of human existence can become the mainspring of an idea of inward or spiritual freedom. A classic example is Sophocles' drama of King Oedipus; sightless, he gains sudden insight, a "shock of recognition."

The intellectually "formidable" social philosopher Hannah Arendt reflected on human nature and the human condition in similar terms:

> The problem of human nature, the Augustinian *quaestio mihi factus sum* ("a question I have become for myself"), seems unanswerable in both its individual psychological sense and its general philosophical sense. It is highly unlikely that we, who can know, determine, and define the natural essences of all things surrounding us, which we are not, should ever be able to do the same for ourselves—this would be like jumping over our own shadow. . . . On the other hand, the conditions of human existence—life itself, natality and mortality, worldliness, plurality, and the earth—can never "explain" what we are or answer the question of who we are for the simple reason that they never condition us absolutely.[8]

The question of tragedy is often asked in an abstract way; for instance, "Why do bad things happen to good people?" The question arises because of the common assumption that God is just and justice rewards goodness with good fortune. But "good things" are not the reward of goodness; goodness produces good things and becomes, in this way, its own reward. Goodness is a spiritual, not a material, reality. The question of life's justice becomes answerable only when we reexamine our assumptions about the moral governance of the world. In the end we must ask: How will I play to the hand that life deals me?

The question of evil is also posed in an abstract, unanswerable way when we ask, "Is human nature good or evil?"— that is, "basically" or "essentially" good or evil? If we mean "necessarily" or "by innate propensity" good or evil, then at the existential level our answer does not matter, for in either case personal responsibility is canceled. "The Devil made me do it" is not a valid excuse. Terms like "essential" are ambiguous; it would be better to speak of "learned propensity."

More fruitful than speculations about human nature are descriptions of the human condition—observing the psychic and social forces, such as "love," that play upon us. Children, whether they are fully loved or deprived of love, grow up craving love. How much love is enough? The question admits of no definite answer. Mature love means wanting the good of another, the beloved, as much as (or even more than) one wants it for oneself. But we inherit from childhood a propensity to reverse the equation, demanding that one be loved as precondition of giving love, and this distortion of mature love can have tragic consequences. The desire *to be loved* more than *to love*, carried to its logical extreme, was deftly described by W. H. Auden as a craving for something we cannot finally have: "Not universal love / But to be loved alone." ("September 1, 1939.")

Similarly, the Reverend John Buehrens, President of the Unitarian Universalist Association, speaks of the universality of narcissism, a distorted and truncated form of love. If evil is a tragic distortion of an original, given good, as Auden's lines suggest, choosing the good is our responsibility even though self-centeredness is a propensity "bred in the bone." Rather than "original sin" I would speak of "original responsibility."

Saying humans are essentially good banks on "idealism," an optimism that tends to slide into sentimentalism; saying we are essentially evil banks on "realism," a pessimism that tends to slide into cynicism. Both answers about "people in general" or "human nature as such" are abstract and ambiguous. They do not start from personal experience, a concrete human situation. They leave us vulnerable to losing heart, losing courage, losing hope.

Taking Evil Seriously

It is difficult to get to the heart of the matter. The human condition is not amenable to rational analysis. Existence is a hard material that resists the penetration of ideas; fact often defeats thought.[9] Thus we never begin life with a clean slate and always live with the dead weight of the past—ancient injustices, hatreds, and patterns of self-defeat. The thirst for revenge is not easily expunged. Evil is radical because it feeds on injured pride and on self-deception. Being opportunistic by nature, it plays on our weaknesses, our prejudices, and our fears. It is always eager to justify itself. Evil is not merely the product of malicious or sick individuals; it is the product of malignant societies. It perpetuates and enlarges itself by eliciting loyalty to its cause, and thus takes on a life of its own. Those who try to fix, to cure, or somehow to undo evil often meet disillusionment, for they did not count the cost; they underestimated the enemy.

Practical-minded people would rather talk about problems to be solved than about evils to be faced and defeated. But problem-solving techniques are not much use in the face of evil, because evil is radical and only an equally radical good will can overcome it: "Blessed are the pure in heart."[10] The radical demands of Jesus' ethic are rooted in this recognition.

One Sunday, speaking as a pulpit guest far from home, I gave a sermon titled "Reckoning With Evil, Counting Our Blessings." It commemorated James Reeb, the Unitarian Universalist minister who became a martyr to the civil rights struggle when he was murdered in Selma, Alabama. The point of my message was our need, in contemporary struggles for social justice, to redeem goodness in the face of evil, to oppose evil without taking on the face of the enemy. A man approached me after the service and said that he was startled by my theme. The idea of evil, he said, hardly ever arose in his church! "It's an awfully harsh word," he said. "Wouldn't it be better to deal with problems that, with intelligence, effort, and good will, will yield solutions?"

The answer is no, not if that means reducing the spiritual question to a practical question, as if "it goes without saying" that we are good. Reasonableness, devoted effort, and selfless goodness are *not* givens of human character; they are achievements. They require us to count the costs and to choose deliberately. That is what Jim Reeb did; we are awed by the memory that the "reward" he received was death. So too, we honor him for his courageous good will, going far beyond what most of us have done.

After Optimism

Liberals, religious or otherwise, would rather deal with the brighter side of life. Liberals tend to believe that, given a chance, people will make the best of things. Liberals favor freedom and change because they be-lieve that, given freedom, people will change the world, even themselves, for the better. Conservatives hold the opposite view: give people freedom and they'll mess things up, including themselves. Both stances, carried to extremes, tend to break down. Irving Kristol acerbically defined a neoconservative as "a liberal who has been mugged."[11]

Did you ever unburden angry or agonized feelings to a friend, seeking sympathy and support, and instead receive practical suggestions about how to solve your problem, complete with an explanation of why these things happen, or why you felt this way? That's when you *really* get angry! What we want above all is an acknowledgment of reality as we experience it. We want our experience to be validated.

Things tend to go swimmingly for liberals in happy times, when problems yield to reasonable solutions, and consensus is readily formed. They tread water when times are bleak, when the populace is polarized, when problems resist solutions. The twentieth century has made liberalism ripe for a dose of existentialism. From existentialism we can learn that human possibilities fully appear only when human limits are fully acknowledged, that heroes shine the brightest when the human condition is darkest, that all problems do not yield to reasonable solutions, that human goodness depends on a transformation of human will.

Good and evil, before they are individual deeds, are lines defining the human condition itself. Historical forces carry us, like the tide, beyond conscious control. Good and evil are what we experience under their pressure. The world presses us, distends us, impassions us. So long as the weather seems to favor us, we give the inner weather of our lives hardly a second thought. We are tragically forgetful not only of others but also of ourselves; we are simply too self-absorbed to notice. However, when we find ourselves at the storm center, victims caught in tragic circumstance, explanations sound like feeble attempts to "explain away." What we know is what we experience.

On our way to visit the neighbors who had lost their son to a drunk driver, Barbara said, "A death is something awful." Our first task is simply to acknowledge the feeling, not to rush to explain it or even assuage it. "The answer" must lie within, not outside, the pain; it requires *compassion*. In the aftermath of tragic loss or shameful failure, talk of how we might prevent such bad things from happening again has the ring of un-reality. What we need to do is to weep for what has been irreparably lost, to weep with those who weep, to weep "the tears that clarify the eye toward charity" (Nemerov).

Human Finitude

We tend to soft-pedal our own pain and anger. We fear that taking evil *too* seriously will undercut the human effort to do good. We even fear that calling it an ineradicable element of life may seem to justify and passively accept evil. To be sure, this darkest aspect of human existence yields no simple answers. But by this late date in "the age of anxiety" (Auden), it should be clear that a rosy view of human nature is defenseless against radical outbreaks of evil. Our century is marred by two notorious cases, Nazism and Communism. The Nazis generated the holocaust of the Jews and other "impure" elements in the name of "freedom" for the German people.[12] Similarly, the Communists justified totalitarianism and brutal repression in the name of a utopian vision of the future. A realistic view of human nature guards against the disillusionment that regularly follows the failure of utopias, Communist or capitalist.[13]

To acknowledge tragedy and evil and not lose heart—to suffer and yet sustain a confident good will—requires of us a deeper understanding of the human condition. We never begin with a clean slate; rather, it is up to us to clean our personal slates when and as we can, to make a new beginning again and again. We are "born free" but we are thrust immediately into history. Thus Abraham Lincoln meditated on history and called for "a new birth of freedom." Thus Paul Tillich named our condition "finite freedom," and our need, a New Being.

We are free, Tillich said, but finite. We have untold possibilities, but we are limited by our own cultural myopia and physical frailty, by the fallibility of our moral judgments and the fear of our own mortality. We tend to deny reality, behaving as if we were an exception to the rules that govern ordinary mortals, such as drinking and driving. Counselors often note a connection between depression and a denial of reality as it impinges on the depressed person. The denial makes one feel better for a while, but eventually, as our denials are exposed to reality, depression takes over. Imagining ourselves to be exceptions to the human condition is the stuff tragedies are made of.

When we overreach our limits, we become tragic figures in the human drama. But equally, we are comic, because our overreaching is the stuff of parody. James Luther Adams described an "existentialist" dive in the Paris of the 1940s: everything was painted black, the music was weird, the refreshments were dark concoctions served on coffins. We enjoy the very thought of such a place: It is a stage for the human comedy.

Keeping Faith

There is more to the story of my neighbor. I did not note, at the outset, *why* I joined MADD. I did so in respect for my neighbor's moral and spiritual witness. I do not argue with her faith; I have never imagined a God who was in control of everything that happened on earth and could be counted on as a cosmic protector. My faith may not be as vulnerable as hers, and yet, like her, I am troubled by the tragic loss and baffled by senseless evil. I too must ask, What goodness and strength sustain me in the face of these things?

First, I recognize that I too am an incurably religious being. I seek to bind myself to that which bestows wholeness and peace, especially when these qualities are wrested from me.

Second, I seek to name God even in dire and painfully difficult circumstances. With compassion, I will do what I can to bring comfort to a suffering family.

Third, I seek to make peace with myself and my God. Our conceptions of God must grow or else be shattered. Meeting the limits of our endurance and understanding, we discover the seriousness of our freedom. We are ready to turn toward the creative freedom of the human spirit.

It is not my business to question, correct, or improve my neighbor's faith, nor to explain how she came to terms with losing her son, after the fateful conjunction of a drunk driver's irresponsibility and her son's being in the wrong place (or was it "the right place"?) for the right reason. But I have reason to believe that, as she moved through the crisis that this death forced upon her, she grew spiritually. She has became a leader in Mothers Against Drunk Driving. An activist response to personal tragedy is not an uncommon phenomenon; entering into a social cause redeems the loss, in some measure, through dedication to the common good. The response transforms grief into outrage, a humanizing anger. She made a new beginning, and I wanted to honor her for it.

4

Creative Freedom

Do we have a human vocation?

You, my friends, were called to be free; only do not turn your freedom into license for your lower nature, but be servants to one another in love. For the whole law can be summed up in a single commandment: "Love your neighbor as yourself."

St. Paul, Galatians 5 : 13–14
(Revised Standard Version)

We must start in religion from our own souls. In these is the fountain of all divine truth. An outward revelation is only possible and intelligible on the ground of conceptions and principles previously furnished by the soul. Here is our primitive teacher and light. Let us not disparage it. . . . The only God whom our thoughts can rest on and our hearts can cling to, and our consciences can recognize, is the God whose image dwells in our own souls.

William Ellery Channing (1780–1842)[1]

For Channing, as for Paul centuries before him, freedom is a positive spiritual and social-ethical reality. Breathing his age's spirit of heroic idealism, Channing could move directly from a spiritual conception of freedom, in the passage cited above, to a political ideal and cause:

> Reverence for liberty, for human rights [is] a sentiment which has grown with my growth, which is striking deeper root in my age, which seems to me a chief element of true love for mankind. . . . I have lost no occasion for expressing my deep attachment to liberty in all its forms . . . and of giving utterance to my abhorrence of all the forms of oppression.

The drive for freedom from ancient religious taboos and dogmas has linked the idea of freedom to the secularization of modern life, that is, the excising of religious sentiments from public life. However, the demand for individual freedom has increasingly come also to be heard as destructive of the social fabric. Liberals and conservatives may want "freedom from" different things, but they are alike troubled by the implications of this now-commonplace observation. Channing could still speak of "reverence for liberty" and identify the feeling as a religious "sentiment," because he lived before the full force of secularization and its corollary, the privatization of religion, were felt. But when the idea of freedom is shorn of all spiritual content—when it is made into a formal condition, a right to do whatever one wishes—it is one step away from self-destruction.

Freedom and Resistance

Political freedom is an external condition of life, an absence of imposed directives and constraints; personal freedom is an internal condition, and requires a capacity for self-direction and self-restraint. We would like to enjoy both conditions and believe that they go hand in hand. However, it often happens that when we enjoy political freedom, we take personal freedom for granted. We squander our freedom with mediocrity, conformism, and sensationalism, as the mass media amply show. Conversely, when we are deprived of external, political, or social freedom, we may discover new depths of internal, personal freedom.

Freedom is often experienced, then, as a capacity to transcend and overcome external constraints, even when repression is most severe. The discovery of the self-transcending power of freedom—the capacity to affirm and renew our humanity in the face of dehumanizing conditions—underlies William Ellery Channing's idea of spiritual freedom.

The psychotherapist Viktor E. Frankl names "spiritual freedom" as the capacity for an inner life of meaning, something that enabled him to survive under the direst imaginable conditions—captivity in a Nazi concentration camp.

In spite of the enforced physical and mental primitiveness of life in a concentration camp, it was possible for spiritual life to deepen. Sensitive people were able to retreat from their terrible surroundings to a life of inner riches and spiritual freedom. . . .

A thought crossed my mind: I didn't even know if my wife were still alive. I knew only one thing: Love goes very far beyond the physical person of the beloved. It finds its deepest meaning in our spiritual being, our inner self. Whether or not [the beloved] is actually present ceases to be of importance. "Set me as a seal upon thy heart, for love is as strong as death." (Song of Songs 8 : 6) . . .

One evening, when we were already resting on the floor of our hut, dead tired, soup bowls in hand, a fellow prisoner rushed in and asked us to run out to the assembly grounds to see the sunset! Standing outside we saw sinister clouds glowing in the west and the whole sky alive with clouds of ever-changing shapes and colors, from steel blue to blood red. The desolate gray mud huts provided a sharp contrast, while the puddles on the muddy ground reflected the glowing sky. Then, after minutes of moving silence, one prisoner declared,

"How beautiful the world *could* be!"[2]

Frankl identifies two capacities, to sustain love and to respond to beauty, as enabling him to resist dehumanization and survive in the concentration camp. Our commonplace notion of "the survival of the fittest" was for him far from the whole story. Notably, he understood survival as a moral and spiritual issue, for it takes more than physical strength to preserve one's humanity. His experiences of beauty and love defined a realm where life was determined not by others but by himself. Personal freedom, Frankl testifies, is a capacity for self-determination, standing against determination by external forces.

The Social Context of Freedom

When we describe a real-life situation, the distinction between personal and social freedom breaks down, for it is in regard to other persons, a social context, that we exercise our freedom, for good or for ill. And just here, in our relation to other persons, a difficulty arises.

It seems presumptuous to generalize, as Frankl does and as we all do, from our own personal experience to the experience of others. For what do we really know about the appreciations or responses of others to beauty or love? The deepest mystery of life seems to be bound up with other persons. I may know something of myself, but I have no way of penetrating the inner life of other persons except as they reveal themselves to me. This recognition of the "otherness" of other persons is the bedrock of "respect." Respect for the dignity of human personality is the basis of dealing truthfully and justly with others. This is why manipulative personalities are so exasperating; they are forever contriving to use others for their own ends, and they drive us crazy. Always treat others as ends in themselves, Immanuel Kant said, and never as means to an end; that is, don't manipulate.

The recognition that another person presents an absolute limit to my understanding and my will is the point at which moral and spiritual awareness are born. Isolated or estranged from others, I cannot act with good purpose. Paradoxically, recognition of the "otherness" of other persons comes before our recognition of their "likeness." Love itself is born of this strange transaction: the willing self-revelation and self-giving of another to yourself, and of yourself to the other. The moment of breakthrough—when strangers become friends, or the estranged become reconciled—is the moment of mutual recognition. With it comes a sense of freedom akin to an end of exile.

This love is the full expression of what Frankl, like Channing, called spiritual freedom. I call it creative freedom, the heart and soul of our calling as human beings, our human vocation.

Recently I was asked to submit a "thought on life" to appear along with a biographical listing in *Who's*

Who in Religion. My first thought was that this had more to do with getting me to buy the book at the special prepublication price than with my being a notable, quotable "who" in religion! But as Oscar Wilde said, "Flattery will get you everywhere," and I proceeded to write this testament to the world:

> I pray for wisdom and courage enough to be able, in the face of any situation, to exercise creative freedom. And how drastically the term, "any situation," qualifies the aspiration! For this includes not only my own frailty, fallibility, and final mortality, but also, and more decisively, my relationship to other persons, who are likewise bearers of the image of God.

My "thought on life" may be as convoluted as a cauliflower but, as Churchill once ungrammatically announced, "It's me."

The central self-recognition of humanity is that we are free. We are free to create or to destroy, and we do both all the time. What, then, will give morally stable direction to this awesome power to do as we will? Only this: a deep sense of vocation as humans and as practitioners of our special callings.

Do we humans possess a human vocation, a calling that we hold in common with all other persons, on the one hand, and uniquely express as individuals, on the other? Yes.

Resacrifying "Vocation"

The word "vocation," from the Latin, *vocatio*, has a curious history. The idea has ancient, Judaic roots. "Moses, Moses, where are you?" calls the voice from the unconsumed burning bush. "Here am I," Moses answers, ready to be sent. Moses, clearly, had a calling.[3]

In the Middle Ages, only priests, monks, and nuns had "callings"; vocations were for "the religious." Everybody else lived within the secular realm and simply worked for a living—or, if they were among the lucky few, lived like aristocrats. Then came Martin Luther, rebelling against the churchly monopoly of God's blessings; he did so in the name of the theological principle of justification by faith alone (*sola fide*). Luther rejected the belief that heavenly merits are imputed to us on account of "good works," deeds of mercy or piety. In the medieval Catholic system, good works accrued especially to members of religious orders or to those doing works of penance at the direction of a priest; it had become a system of ecclesiastical control. Luther declared that in the sight of God all honest labor is dignified; all vocations are blessed by God— all, at least, except thievery, banking, and other dishonorable callings.

It is fascinating to read Luther's shocked words about the Fuggers, the wealthiest banking house of his age. The very idea of multiplying money by money-lending rather than by what he considered honest labor, baffled and scandalized him.[4] He considered interest-taking a trick of the Devil. We smile at his naiveté—or did, until the recent junk bond, leveraged buyout, and savings and loan debacles reminded us of our own naiveté about greed. Luther's attitude shows how little he understood the forces of secularization that were already at work in his age. His universalization of vocation represents a victory for human dignity. But it had unintended consequences, because with the fading of religious fervor, "vocation" was desacrified. If every honest labor equally represents a divine calling, then perhaps none does. In the modern era secularization progressively sweeps the field; now vocation is just another name for a career.

In his extensive writings on the concept, James Luther Adams has sought to renew the spiritual and moral import of "vocation," applying it to the professions, to social institutions, and to the individual person.[5] To speak of "human vocation" is to emphasize the need to have a fundamental purpose in life—a "good work" to which your life is given. Vocation is more than a personal-ethical concept. Because social institutions mediate and shape our human vocations, it is also a social-ethical concept. Your vocation is fulfilled through skills and labors that serve the purposes of the human community. Work as gainful employment is an important part of our lives, but it is only a part. Life itself is the whole.

So we come full circle. The original, religious meaning of "vocation" needs to be recovered, not in the medieval sense that sets one apart from the world, "under holy orders," but in the sense of service to the social good. To speak of vocation is to recognize anew the dignity of every form of work, whether in the marketplace, the factory or the fields, the public agency, the home, the voluntary association, the school, the church, or the art studio. Each can contribute to the common good.

Many people live within highly constricted arenas of life. They live for their careers. And if they are devoted also to their families—the commonly stated justification for being focused on the job to the exclusion of community concerns—they consider themselves entirely virtuous.[6] Such a privatized existence fails to recognize the ways in which the well-being of the family itself depends on the complex network of social institutions in a healthy community. For this reason James Luther Adams has emphasized our responsibility to participate in voluntary associations working for social well-being and reform. A healthy democracy depends on the independence and the courageous efforts of voluntary associations; to take active part in them is our vocation as citizens in a democracy.

When we enlarge the arena of our lives to include the public world, our work takes on a deeper meaning as well. A chief virtue of the church is to invite people into the larger world of concern for others, including both the human family and the natural world we share with all creatures. A religious community asks, Are you committed to something beyond yourself? Such commitment, it reminds us, is central to our human vocation, for through it we express the very meaning of our humanity.

Being in the Image of God

According to Genesis 1, the biblical hymn of beginnings, God is the original creative artist. On the sixth day God created the land animals—everything from what our children call creepy-crawlies to what we think of as the highest animals, ourselves! It seems surprising, then, that no special day is reserved for the creation of humans. But in the biblical view human beings are one among the great variety of animals, all of whom are imbued with breath, understood as God's life-giving Spirit. The principle is clear: Fundamentally, all animals on earth are created equal.

And yet, the story also recognizes that humans are an odd case among the animals:

God said, "Let us make man in our image, after our likeness; and let them have dominion over the fish of the sea, and over the birds of the air, and over the cattle, and over all the earth, and over every creeping thing that creeps upon the ground according to its kind." And God saw that it was good. So God created man in his own image, in the image of God he created him; male and female he created them. (Genesis 1 : 26–27, Revised Standard Version)

That the passage speaks of "man" in the singular, and then of "them" in the plural, indicates that the text refers not to a single, mythic, first ancestor, but to the human collectivity, "humankind." That the singular biblical God here speaks of himself as "us" may indicate that, originally, "he" was chairperson of a committee; but more likely it is simply the royal "we."

In our time, this has become a controversial passage, for two reasons. First, up to the final phrase, it sounds thoroughly male centered. Yahweh tended to talk that way, according to the priestly authors, no doubt all of whom were men. But perhaps "male and female he created them" was a first, blushing attempt to remove a glaring sex-bias! I give the priestly authors of Genesis 1 the benefit of the doubt: even they recognized that, in principle, "the image of God" is reflected equally in woman and man.[7]

One person commented to me recently that, if we are made in the image of God, God must be as venial or even vicious as we are. The logic is impeccable, but the premise is cynical. Genesis invites us to place a positive value on all creation, even humans, for it says, again and again, "God saw all that he had made, and it was good." On these terms, our sins and shortcomings should be viewed as tragic (or perhaps tragicomic) distortions of the divine image. Humanity's original directive is toward the good.

The biblical idea of creation rules out the possibility of an ultimate dualism. Evil must have some other explanation than the supposition of two ultimate principles or powers—good and evil, or God and Satan—locked in combat to the end of time. This view is morally and spiritually dangerous, because it promotes a rejection of the world; mythically speaking the world is said to be under Satan's rule. It also rules out considering the human body or any other aspect of the natural world inherently corrupt, or alien to our spiritual natures. Rather, in the maxim of medieval theology, "Being as such is good."

Genesis Chapter 1 is controversial for a second reason as well. As our concern for preserving the natural environment grows, it is sometimes said that the Bible has invited a fantastic human arrogance; by giving the human being "dominion" over all the other creatures, the story legitimates domination in the form of a destructive exploitation of the natural world. Often this argument seems to be an attempt to find somebody else to blame for our ecological troubles. A more thoughtful reading of the passage points in the opposite direction—an interpretation supporting our moral responsibility for the natural world.

When Genesis says that the human being is made "in the image of God," it cannot mean in a physical likeness; it means precisely the capacity to exercise a God-like "dominion," that is, ruling with a God-like creative power and good will. I abbreviate this complex idea of the *imago dei*, the image of God in which we are made, as "creative freedom." (I do not say *were* made, but *are* made, that is, are continuously made and remade; we must use it or lose it.) Dominion is something we humans inescapably have; to talk as if we could shuck it off and return to "a state of nature" is another form of irresponsibility.[8] Romanticizing nature is at best irrelevant. The natural world is our human responsibility, within a covenant founded in love and gratitude. To ignore or deny this responsibility is to refuse to take the imperatives of the environmental movement seriously. The question is not whether we will exercise dominion, but how, to what ends, with what wisdom and care for the earth?

This is the defining mark of our human vocation: to use power responsibly, to work for the common good, to create. We have within us the capacity to exercise a God-like creative freedom.

Choosing and Being Chosen

The biblical idea of being "chosen" is closely related to the ideas of vocation and spiritual freedom. This idea also gives us difficulty, since it too seems to invite arrogance.[9] But consider the way in which the sense of being chosen occurs in the following personal prayer, which a parishioner gave me recently after a long conversation:

> God grant me vision to see the road you have put before me, strength to walk it, and fortitude to complete the journey. Have patience with me, for I am easily distracted and often tempted to stray. Yet I know that when I stay on my own path I find peace, even when the journey is difficult. So, when I am tired and frustrated, please remind me of why I was chosen. Amen.

When we enter into times of solitary self-reflection, the sense of being called, chosen, sent, comes up again and again. It is also reflected in the words of the late Secretary General of the United Nations, Dag Hammarskjold:

> I don't know Who—or what—put the question. I don't know when it was put. I don't even remember answering. But at some moment I did answer *Yes* to Someone—or Something—and from that hour I was certain that existence is meaningful and that, therefore, my life, in self-surrender, had a goal. From that moment I have known what it means "not to look back" and "to take no thought for the morrow." . . . After that . . . nothing could be taken from me.[10]

This meditation on a fundamental turning point in his

life led Hammarskjold to hold onto the integrity of his own soul in a way that the world could never take from him. It is interesting to note, here, that Hammarskjold does not say that he *first* discovered the meaning of life and *then* decided that his life had a meaning, a goal. His intensely personal *yes* is a starting point, an "original decision." It affirms his creative freedom, his part in the creation of a meaning that transcends himself.

Answering to Life

Viktor Frankl's report of his triumph over despair in a Nazi death camp and the meaning he forged from the experience is equally striking. His was the direst human condition, living where human dignity was held in absolute contempt. "Be useful to our war machine or die" was the only meaning that the masters of the concentration camp allowed. But using the sovereign power of his freedom to create meaning, Frankl chose the terms of his own survival—as a human being, never as a mere tool. Here he reflects on what he learned in the concentration camp:

> Woe to him who saw no more sense in his life, no aim, no purpose, and therefore no point in carrying on. He was soon lost. [Those who] rejected all encouraging arguments [would typically say], "I have nothing to expect from life any more." What

sort of answer can one give to that? What was needed was a fundamental change in our attitude toward life. We had to learn . . . that it did not really matter what we expected from life, but rather what life expected from us. We needed to stop asking about the meaning of life, and instead think of ourselves as those who were being questioned by life—daily and hourly. . . . Life ultimately means taking the responsibility to . . . fulfill the tasks which it constantly sets for [us].

We are saved, Frankl said, by beauty and by love. These wonders of life call to us, even in the darkest moments of despair. They call us to give our lives a purpose, whatever our circumstances, and through them to create meaning.

I pray that I may be loving and wise enough to exercise creative freedom, whatever the condition of my life. My own frailties and fears limit my abilities; yet may I "fear no evil" (Psalm 23 : 4), but act in strength and courage. Other persons also limit my power to do as I will; yet may I see and honor the divine image in them, and so enlarge my own humanity.

This, then, is the point at which we turn from *understanding* the human condition to *deciding* our human vocation. We say: I will take responsibility for the tasks of the common good to which I am called. And when I cry out for help, will life answer me? Yes—in beauty and in love.

The Moral Covenant

Are ethical values rooted in reality?

Human beings, individually and collectively, become human by making commitments, by making promises. The human being, as such, Martin Buber says, is the promise-making, promise-keeping, the promise-breaking, promise-renewing creature. . . . The covenant includes a rule of law, but it is not fundamentally a legal covenant. It depends on faithfulness, and faithfulness is nerved by loyalty, by love. . . . Ultimately the ground of faithfulness is the divine and human love that will not let us go.

James Luther Adams[1]

The possible redemption from the predicament of irreversibility . . . is the faculty of forgiving. The remedy for unpredictability . . . is contained in the faculty to make and keep promises. The two faculties belong together in so far as one of them, forgiving, serves to undo the deeds of the past, . . . and the other, binding oneself through promises, serves to set up in the ocean of uncertainty . . . islands of security. . . .

Hannah Arendt, *The Human Condition*[2]

It would not be hard to make the case that we live within a moral chaos, a world impassioned by a million hatreds and fears, and marred by every one of the seven deadly sins. But how do you make the case that, nevertheless, we live within a moral covenant—a web of promises that are, at once, inescapable and freely chosen?

The Covenant-Making Animal

Covenants create relationships of mutual responsibility. They do so not by nature (as, for instance, by childbirth) but by voluntary decision of the parties to them. We may violate our covenants, but we cannot escape "covenanting" itself. In the fundamental sense of the idea suggested by James Luther Adams, covenants constitute our very humanity (our moral being). Aristotle named the human being "the political animal"; in Martin Buber's paraphrase, we are the promising animal. If so, the principle of covenant is inescapable in human existence. It is something we cannot not do and remain human. Nevertheless, an act of covenanting, a mutual promising, entails freedom. Actual covenants are historically enacted; they are the acts of particular parties in particular times and places. We may either affirm or escape, keep or betray, our actual covenants; they are chosen, revised, and renewed in again and again.

I am suggesting that "covenant" is both a descriptive and a prescriptive principle in human life. It bridges the gap between our being and our doing, between ontology and ethics, between "isness" and "oughtness."[3] The moral chaos we experience is an absence, or a distortion, or a denial, or a violation, or even a willful destruction, of the moral covenant that underlies it. In one sense we cannot "destroy" what is rooted in moral reality; in another sense—when we destroy the trust that others have in this reality—we can.

Moral Disorder

Consider the disorder of our daily experience of the world. In the first chapter I cited the story of Thomas Sutherland, one of the last American hostages to be released from captivity in Lebanon. The following items were other events broadcast that same day on *All Things Considered*[4]:

- The US Supreme Court's voiding of the New York "Son of Sam" law, which had prevented criminals from profiting from the sale of their stories—the case in point being one Henry Hill and his publisher, Simon and Schuster. In their interview Mr. Hill said that while he had never himself killed anyone, he had been present when murders were committed. After all, he said, "violence is a part of that life."

- The stalled Arab–Israeli peace talks, because of the refusal of the Israelis to meet with Palestinian delegation, lest it be implied that they have a right to exist.

- The conviction of four teenagers for murdering Brian Watkins, a young tourist from Utah, in a New York subway.

- William Kennedy Smith telling his story, on trial for rape, and his being asked by the prosecutor if he were "some kind of sex machine."[5]

- Patrick Buchanan's decision to run for the presidency of United States on an "Americans First" and "let's end the welfare state" platform that he describes as "a religious and cultural war."

- The continuing, bloody, civil war in the former Yugoslavia, while the United States, like rest of the world, sits back and watches.

- New concerns about the disposition of nuclear weapons in the Ukraine: to be destroyed, sold, or kept?

- A mass murder in the small town of California, Missouri—one of several in the news recently.

- The award of the Nobel Peace prize, *in absentia*, to Aung San Suu Kyi, who was under house arrest for anti-government activities in Burma (Myamar).

- Long, painful interviews with workers who lost their jobs when the Brockway glass factory was closed in Ada, Oklahoma, after the New York investment firm, Kohlberg, Kravits, had engineered a leveraged buyout. The takeover of the parent company, Owens-Illinois Glass, was illegal, according to *All Things Considered*, but unlikely to be contested by the administration of President George H. Bush.

Such is our daily fare. Each item in this miscellany involves grave moral issues, and each makes us (if I do not assume too much) shudder with outrage. It would be interesting to count the occurrence, among these items, of the Seven Deadly Sins—pride, wrath, greed, gluttony, lust, envy, sloth. From this day's temperature reading of the moral health of the world, only gluttony seems to be missing.

Moral Virtues

What of the Four Cardinal Virtues—prudence, temperance, fortitude, and justice? Auug San Suu Kyi exemplified them to the highest degree. Clearly she is a woman of fortitude and justice. We might question whether she could be called prudent or temperate; nevertheless, her decision to engage in a hunger protest was not suicidal, but a risk calculated to achieve international attention. I would call her prudent and temperate in the best senses of those terms. She knew the likely consequences of her actions and chose to act in spite of them.

Thomas and Jean Sutherland also exemplify surpassing virtues. His wife, Jean, said of the ordeal:

> Sometimes it has to be that someone says, "OK, you did this to me; I did this to you. You did this to me; I did this to you," and when you have had that piled up over thousands of years, sometimes someone has to say, "Let's break it, and let's break it right here." . . . We as Americans must see this, and we must be the leaders in saying, "Let's go forward from here and go for peace."

We might identify the underlying moral qualities of Jean Sutherland's words as faith, hope, and love, the virtues named in 1 Corinthians 13 : 13. Christian tradition calls them "theological virtues" because they go beyond achievement by human will, unaided by

divine grace. Whatever their source, lacking these qualities—courage, intelligence, or any other virtue we might
name—is easily tinged with arrogance; in this sense
faith, hope, and love may be named transcendental
virtues—virtues that enable other virtues to be truly
virtuous.

Auug San Suu Kyi's and Jean Sutherland's moral
stances are markedly different. But they also reveal a
symmetry, suggesting a complementary of virtues
within the moral covenant. Auug San Suu Kyi coura-
geously demanded freedom and respect for her people,
the Burmese. She did so by exercising her own freedom
and self-respect, in spite of the punishment she would
suffer in consequence. Jean Sutherland, freeing herself
from the spirit of revenge, appealed for reconciliation
and a renewal of community, in spite of the evil, the
gross violation of humanity, done to her and her husband. She transcended personal outrage for the sake of
her perception of a greater good.

As different as the situations of the two women
were, both exemplified a creative freedom acting to
uphold and renew the moral covenant. In one sense
the covenant is inescapable, and in another sense it
de-pends on our courageous choosing. It is a transcendental structure in which personal freedom and mutual
respect validate and support each other.

CHAPTER FIVE

Beyond Absolutism and Relativism

On what basis can we assert "this is right" and "this is wrong"? That is, what validates any ethical standard or particular ethical judgment? The question has been subject to endless contention. Consider the tension between the absolutist and the relativist stances in ethics.

The absolutist says, "Right is what authority says is right; it is obedience to the moral law." In popular imagination God is the giver of moral law; the story of Moses receiving the Ten Commandments on Mt. Sinai dramatizes the idea. The appeal of moral absolutism tends to grow in times of moral chaos; people say, "You simply have to declare what's right and punish wrongdoers." Absolutisms are brittle and tend to break down in the face of social change; they are upheld by enclaves that seek to insulate themselves from "worldly influences."

The relativist position is more complex. It sees right and wrong as relative to the situation; absolute or universal moral laws do not exist. The argument takes various forms. "Cultural relativism" looks at the diversity of human cultures and says that "right" is what serves the needs and traditions of any given social system. (This view is a staple of college courses. Being popular in "counterculture" cultures, it seems to me to be rather "culturally relative" itself.)

"Situation ethics" is another form of moral relativism; the right or wrong of any decision, it is said, depends on your personal situation. However, the "situationism" of Joseph Fletcher, its leading proponent, is only *relatively* relative, since he holds that all decisions are to be made with respect to a single, overriding moral value, love.[6] Already in ancient times St. Augustine stated the rule: "Love and do what you will." The basis of this singular value is unclear, unless it is the Christian affirmation, "God is love"—an absolute.

Yet another form of moral relativism, articulated by contemporary linguistic philosophers, is called "emotivism." It asserts that statements about what is good or right amount to statements of feeling or personal preference; beyond this they have no empirical or rational content. Popularly expressed, emotivism says, "If it feels good, do it."

One sees in these relativisms the privatization of ethics, either from the attempt to cope with the dissolution of traditional constraints or from the desire to be free of them altogether. But neither they nor the absolutisms they seek to displace are wholly convincing. Is there a way beyond the impasse between these two contrary views of ethics? I believe there is and have named it "covenantal ethics."[7]

Critical Realism

The first question for ethics is not the question of the

validity or the source of norms; it is the question of the person facing a decision: How can I make a good decision? Norms may help guide the decision, but they cannot determine it, for the person must still decide *whether* or *how* the norm applies, or even *which* of several possibly conflicting norms applies. Our freedom makes "relativists" of us all. And yet, we are never absolutely free, for we must still act in accord with fundamental purposes or goals. We do so because these aims promise fulfillment of a vision of life, or accord with our sense of human vocation.

There is, then, a dimension of moral necessity within which our moral freedom is acted out. From birth onward, we become persons in a community of persons and can only find fulfillment of our needs and desires in community. Good communities seek the voluntary consent of their members. We may *dissent* from our community as often as we need to; we do so in *consent* to a higher order of community, as we conceive it. This is the right of conscience, risky and fallible though it be.

But what is our "community"? It takes many forms, from the family to the "global" community, but what is "it" itself? The largest conceivable community is a spiritual vision that we seek to realize through our community-creating actions. Ecological awareness may lead us to speak of "the interdependent web of existence of which we are a part," one of the Principles of the Unitarian Universalist Association. Awareness of biblical and Western political traditions may lead us to adopt James Luther Adams's term (possibly derived from Jonathan Edwards), "the covenant of being."[8] Such terms suggest a social and relational vision of ultimate reality, that is, of an inescapable dimension of existence. Moral dissent is not anarchic or arbitrary when it is asserted in consent to the moral covenant; that to which we are bound validates our freedom.

These abstract ideas can be made concrete at the level of our personal ethical decisions. Describe, then, an actual human situation that morally concerns you, and ask about it: (1) What troubles my conscience—my sense of the rightness of things—in this situation? (2) How do I understand this situation? What conflicting or contradictory viewpoints are at work? (3) What personal and social values are for me central to this situation, and shape the decisions I make? (4) What active commitments will sustain the common good in this situation, and renew it when it has been violated?[9] To make the matter as concrete as possible, imagine Jean Sutherland or Auug San Suu Kyi in their situations asking themselves these questions.

This process of reflection helps to move us toward a critical realism in ethics. It is *realistic* because it first asks us to describe the situation, and to do so in terms that are both emotional and analytic. It is *critical* because it then asks us to make our own best judgment, in terms the personal values and social purposes we uphold. In this way we heighten consciousness of the moral covenant, the web of promises and agreements that we inescapably live within and recreate in time and history.

Covenants

The idea of covenant comes to us laden with social, political, and religious history. It takes various forms in various contexts; thus a covenant is a kind of agreement, a kind of promise, a kind of commitment, a kind of founding charter, a kind of compact, a kind of testament. Like a contract, a covenant secures the future actions of the parties to it; unlike a contract, a covenant endures as long as their relationship endures. When a covenant hardens into a legal document, it becomes a contract. Unlike a contract, a covenant is an open-ended promise—a commitment to future actions that uphold a vision of the good, yet to be fully understood, yet to be fulfilled. It is a metaphor drawn from social and political experience, and applied to religious and moral experience.

The moral covenants we live within have a spiritual dimension, as we recognize, for instance, when a person makes a promise after having broken other promises: Now trust is in question and undermines the willingness to accept new promises. The moral problem is fairly straightforward: not only to make promises but also to keep them, and not only to keep them but also to improve or enlarge them in the face of new situations. The spiritual problem is fraught with difficulty: not simply to make or improve our promises, but to renew them when they have been broken, recognizing that, at some level, they always have been broken.

The mutual reaffirmation and renewal of covenants, then, is not a problem you solve "once and for all"; it is a continuous moral and spiritual process in human life. To believe that it is possible to renew a covenant after grievous wrongs have been done is a central spiritual issue of human life. The possibility of covenant renewal reveals its sacred dimension; we break our covenants, but the moral covenant itself is a constant basis of moral meaning and value.[10] Religiously speaking: God does not break the covenant; God remains "the love that has laid hold upon us and will not let us go."

The contrast between a covenant and a contract is readily seen in relation to marriage. The relationship must be founded in love and gratitude, rather than the calculation of mutual advantages. Also, the terms of the commitment are open-ended, not finite; they bind our actions for the indefinite future. In the wedding ceremony the couple gives public witness to their commitment to one another, usually in the form of vows or pledges. In the language of the old English marriage service they say, "I plight thee my troth," that is, I pledge to you my truth, my faithfulness.

First and foremost, as James Luther Adams notes, a covenant is a relationship of affection. It is born of love, not law. Secondarily, it is also a "lawful" relationship; for instance, marriage entails moral and legal obligations for both parties. Third, Adams says, a covenant is freely made by the individuals as moral agents, that is, as self-responsible persons. Fourth, we make promises out of "a sense of promise," the fervent belief that good will come of this relationship in the future, more than we presently know.

The cycle is complete. A covenant is motivated by gratitude and love; it is sustained by the keeping of its particular obligations; it is freely made by persons who respect one another; and it is believed in for the promise of a greater good to come.

Ethics Without Virtue?

Marriage most clearly exemplifies this pattern, but every form of human community is made, sustained, and renewed in this way. There are many instances of covenanting in human life. One example is a church that sustains itself by financial commitments of the members, decided by them on the basis of a democratically decided budget. Yet a church is built on more than rights and obligations. It is born of affection and gratitude, and it is sustained by a sense of promise—shared devotion to ends beyond ourselves. A covenantal community calls forth certain virtues, that is, qualities of character, in its members.

"Virtue," an old-fashioned sounding word with a moralistic ring, has fallen into disuse, but recent moral discourse is rehabilitating it.[11] William Raspberry highlighted the reason for this in his column, "Ethics Without Virtue" (*The Washington Post*, December 16, 1991). He cited Professor Christine Hoff Sommers's critique of the ineffectiveness of some methods of ethical education for children. Typically, horrendous moral dilemmas are posed ("You are in a life boat with only enough water for half the people, and you have a gun. Which ones do you throw to the sharks?"), but no particular qualities of human character are upheld as inherently good. It is "ethics without virtue." Whereas "virtues" are meaningful only in relation to an encompassing vision of life, these educational exercises proceed in a moral vacuum. Raspberry concludes, "We used to teach our children (through fable, Bible stories, heroes' lives, and family myths) what ethical behavior—what goodness—was all about. Now we teach them lifeboat dilemmas and wonder why they're not inspired." Indeed, ethics without virtue is empty.

Vital communities celebrate heroes as *our* heroes and extol their virtues. Thus a memorial service for a notable or an especially beloved person becomes an occasion to renew communal bonds. My congregation's service for Joseph L. Fisher, a former member of Congress, a founder and leader of his church, and a former Moderator of the Unitarian Universalist Association, dramatized this phenomenon for me.[12] The stories of peoples' lives are recited to show their excellence and moral character, the commitments they lived for and steadfastly held to through life's trials. These things inspire us. A memorial service can serve the moral education of the community.

The Prophetic Virtues

The prophets of ancient Israel announced qualities of personal and social relationships that sustained and renewed Israel's covenant with Yahweh. I call them the covenantal virtues, for these are the qualities of life that uphold the covenant. They may be expressed differently in different cultures, but they are basically universal. A well-known instance is Micah's question, "What the Lord doth require of thee?" and his answer, "To do justice, and to love mercy [or kindness], and to walk humbly with your God." (Micah 6 : 8) That is, be just in your judgments, be kind and merciful in your actions, and be constant in your sense of humility or reverence. These are the qualities Yahweh "requires." A religious and moral symmetry obtains, for these virtues fulfill the covenant with God by fulfilling the covenantal bond with your neighbors.

Curiously, the Hebrew prophets never recite the Ten Commandments or other moral codes; they never say, "You must obey these absolute laws." Rather, they invoke the qualities of personal and communal life that uphold the covenantal relationship, and they tell the dire consequences of violating them. The prophet Hosea said:

> And I will make for you a covenant on that day
> with the beasts of the field, the birds of the air,
> and the creeping things of the ground, and I will
> abolish the bow, the sword, and war from the land;
> and I will make you lie down in safety. And I will
> betroth you to me for ever; I will betroth you to me
> in righteousness and in justice, in steadfast love,
> and mercy. I will betroth you to me in faithfulness;
> [then] you shall know the Lord. (Hosea 2 : 18–20;
> Revised Standard Version)

The following ideas are found in Hosea's passage: (1)
The covenant is a personal, affectional relationship, not
a legal code. (2) The promise of faithfulness to the
covenant is peace: you will "lie down safely." (3) The
covenant is universal, for it includes not only the
historical realm of human societies, but also the natural realm of the animals. (4) Yahweh's love for his
people is said to be irrevocable: "I will betroth you to
me for ever."

Hosea names several specific covenantal virtues:
righteousness (the opposite of crookedness, or lying),
justice (making just judgments), steadfast love (or con-
stancy in caring), mercy (sometimes called kindness,
sometimes called forgiveness), and faithfulness (or fidelity). As noted above, peace (*shalom* in Hebrew,
meaning both social and personal wholeness) is also
implied. *These qualities of human life are validated as*

morally good because they uphold and renew the moral covenant. Disregarding or betraying them breaks the covenant. In sharpest contrast to a warm "mystical" feeling, *this* is what it means, Hosea concludes, to know God.

Resolving Moral Conflict

Moral realism begins with a description of the moral reality within which we inescapably live. If so, moral values are rooted in "reality"—the social and ecological reality within which we live and move and have our being. They are the intimate and ultimate facts of life. They establish peace.

Some virtues seem to be in conflict with others, and this troubles us. For example, justice and peace seem to be conflicting goals in many political situations, but the familiar slogan states their relationship nicely: "If you want peace, work for justice." This does not solve the practical problem we face, but it may help us resist compromising one goal in favor of the other. For instance, the proposed political settlement in Bosnia in 1993 radically compromised justice. A cessation of warfare which establishes an unjust settlement is a "peace" without *shalom*.

A still more difficult tension arises between justice and love, for justice often seems to require punishment, while love seems to require its opposite, forgiveness. Indeed, the conflict between these two moral purposes is sharp and often seems humanly irreconcilable. But within the moral covenant they modify each other: love reminds us not to confuse just punishment with revenge, and justice reminds us to not to confuse forgiveness with indifference. "Justice" is not just, Paul Tillich said, unless it is "creative justice," that is, justice tempered with mercy in order that a new covenantal bond may be formed. In this way love and justice qualify each other and serve the same end, to renew the covenant.

A report in *The Washington Post*, describing the brutalities to which several hostages held by radical Muslim groups in Lebanon were subjected and the way that the hostages sometimes fought back, suggests that demanding justice may help reestablish relationships that make kindness or mercy possible: "Once, when their keeper 'once too often' dumped their food on their foam mattresses, [former hostage] Alann Steen said, 'We are not dogs!' and smashed it against the wall." The first reaction of their captors was to commit further acts of brutality; but eventually, by taking the risk of standing up for themselves, the captives won more respectful and humane treatment. Although powerless to retaliate, Steen had learned to "fear no evil." The moral covenant was at work.

In another instance, one of the guards who had physically abused the Catholic priest Lawrence Jenco came to him "seeking pardon." Jenco recalled his asking, "Do you forgive me, *Abuna* [father]?" Jenco reported, "I forgave him. It was at this instant, it was intuitous to me, that I would go home because enemies had become brothers." Three months later Father Jenco was released. Did the guard seek forgiveness out of genuine piety? Or was it out of fear that an enemy bent on revenge would be released? Did Jenco grant forgiveness out of recognition that he and his captor, Christian and Muslim, were locked in a symbolic adversity that must not bind their souls forever? Did the Muslim come to see that, too? We do not know the answers to these questions, but clearly, in the events Jenco recalled the moral covenant was at work. Both men recognized their need to consent to it, if they were to live without fear.

Responsibility and Forgiveness

We covenant with others freely, but we can only do so as mutually respecting persons. We are not free to do otherwise. Always, in human life, wrongs have already been done; covenants have already been broken. Relationships have been violated, and hatred has invited a longing for revenge. Therefore, *mirabile dictu*, we can only seek mercy, and when it is sincerely asked of us, we can only give it.

Respect means according to others responsibility for their actions. Forgiveness means releasing them from the moral consequences of their wrongful deeds. We inescapably live within these twin realities. Within the moral covenant, there is a marvelous symmetry.[13]

6

Newmindedness

Is help available when I need it?

A rabbi asked, Does God pray? Another answered, Yes, he prays that his wrath may be turned to mercy.

The Talmud

You will recall the man to whom Jesus said, "This can be done, if you have faith." And the man replied, "I believe, help thou my unbelief." It is as part of the awareness of faith that the sense of the lack of faith arises. The resource that is within us is the clue to the resource that is beyond ourselves, and this we tap in the experience of prayer. . . . I tap the resource that is beyond me by making conscious contact with the resource that is within me. "The beyond is within" is the way Plotinus put it.

Howard Thurman[1]

The day I sat down to write about "newmindedness," I developed a Class A head cold for no apparent reason. It was just the thing to get me *not* in the mood. Where, I asked myself, *did* I pick up this germ? Was it sent by God? "God, what day did you decide to create germs? It must have been after the first seven, after the Fall. Was it a botched biotech experiment, or garden variety mean-spiritedness?"

Only later did I realize how much I was sounding like Jonah under his wilted vine (probably a caster oil plant, the scholars say). I should have been contemplating not *new-* but *old-*mindedness. The Talmud, with its marvelous sense of the humanity of God, suggests a way of getting from "the old" back to "the new"—namely, by way of protest: "May God repent!"

That's the spirit! Yes, but unless God prays, can God repent? Who, then, has God to pray to? Perhaps to us, his wronged creatures.

Learning Humility

An important thing the church does for me—may do for any of us—is help us put such small troubles in perspective. I pay a pastoral visit to a young woman in the hospital; she is seriously ill, and, after my petty complaints, I am shamed by her cheerfulness and her determination to overcome adversity. She speaks easily of herself, and I come to know her intimate fears and hopes in a way that many casual meetings would never reveal.

I wonder: Am I so trustworthy? After I leave I am once again thankful for hospital visits. I come away blessed by those I call upon.

Back at the office, three men come by and ask for money. It's for groceries, they say. I'm impatient and try not to show it. Wary of being taken in by petty con artists, I listen to their story. They are Bolivians. They say they are out of work, and their families are hungry. I am skeptical. I am trying to decide whether I believe their stories. Then I realize that there is a prior question: How much does the truth or the falsity of their stories matter? Their eyes are downcast; they seem unhappy to be asking for help. The idea of probing their veracity begins to embarrass me, and I cut the explanations short; here, human dignity is also at risk. Thanks to the discretionary fund that the church makes available to me, I am able to respond to their need without a lot of red tape, and I do so. Again, it is so easy! Watching them leave, I reflect: How secure my life is by comparison!

So it goes. The church helps me counter the old slippage of the heart into oldmindedness. Which is what? Grumpy ingratitude? A religious community can help us, and often does help us, in this way. This is as it should be, for the church is here to make good, if only in small ways, the immense and seemingly improbable promise of faith: Help is available to us when we need it.

But how will we name the turn of heart and mind that enables this fragile faith to endure in the face of adversity? We seem to have no adequate language for it.

Among all the first questions of the religious quest this one most challenges my heart and mind: Is help available when I need it? Or am I ultimately alone in the universe? "Help" must mean more than a friendly visit in the hospital or emergency financial aid to those in need. It must include the spiritual help we seek when, having nowhere else to turn, we feel driven to prayer.

It seems odd to put the matter that way. But when else would you pray other than when, lacking any other resource, you feel driven to it? Perhaps you or I *ought* to pray when we feel buoyed with thankfulness; perhaps it is a lack of spiritual discipline or reflectiveness that leads us to take good times for granted. Perhaps. I have often reflected—typically at hospital bedsides—that prayers need to begin with giving thanks, for *something*, precisely when gratitude is most difficult to feel. Does giving thanks feel most authentic when it comes the hardest? Yes, because that is when the spirit of self-sufficiency has fled. Few of us are saintly enough to pray in moments of joy. But everyone, I suppose, feels driven to prayer in deeply troubled or dire times, even if, as many say, they "don't believe in prayer."

Faith and prayer are closely related, for both carry us into some misty region beyond ourselves, a realm of dependency. Both seem like crutches to those proud of their independence; the frail, the faulted, and the fallible know they need all the help they can get. Both faith and prayer are so often inauthentic that the wise are wary of them; but the wisest, I believe, affirm them nevertheless. They are not afraid of seeming to be naive, but welcome a childlike "second naiveté."

The Problem of Authenticity

The young people of my church chose, for their recent Youth Sunday service, a one-word theme: "faith." At first I was skeptical about their ability to deal meaningfully with such a broad and basic theme; as it turned out, I was the one of little faith. It was precisely the profound and "open-ended" character of the theme that seemed to elicit from these young people personal, emotionally touching stories. These stories illustrated their experience of faith in many forms: trusting, having confidence, being loyal, believing and wondering, being faithful to ideals. How remarkable, I thought, that these very untraditional Unitarian Universalist high school students would have so many serious and deeply felt things to say about such a traditional religious idea!

One of the young people, Nels Roningen, had an angle of vision that set his presentation apart. Faith is not necessarily good, he said; after all, faith can be fanatical or foolish. Whether it is good or bad, or wise or foolish, depends on what it is you put your faith in. I wanted to shout, Amen! Although his was the most skeptical—the least "religious"—of the several statements on faith, his was also the most sharply insightful.

He provoked rethinking the meaning of the word itself. He recognized the problem of inauthentic or perverse faith, "blind faith" in the service of destructive ends.[2]

Prayer, too, is not necessarily good. It can be self-righteous or self-serving. The prayer of the Pharisee, "I thank thee God that I am not like other men" (Luke 18 : 11) is a classic example of self-righteous prayer. A classic example of self-serving prayer was recalled by Dietrich Bonhoeffer, in prison for his part in a plot on Hitler's life: "It is absurd how one can't help hoping when an air raid is announced, that it will be the turn of other places this time. The principle is the same as that of 'Holy St. Florian, spare my house, and set others on fire.'"[3]

Prayer, like faith, is not necessarily authentic and can take radically inauthentic forms. We might expect prayer to arise from a serene and confident faith, but the opposite seems to be the case. Often prayer is a struggling, almost inarticulate outcry.[4] Paradoxically, authentic prayer is never easy or "confident of reward," but reflects an internal resistance to believing or confidence or faithfulness, something that needs to be overcome. Howard Thurman expresses this insight into the spiritual difficulty of prayer when he says, "It is as part of the awareness of faith that the sense of the lack of faith arises." Faith, aware of its inadequacy, prays that it may be improved, perhaps that its wrath may be turned to mercy. When the act of prayer is a risky or a creative venture, not a "canned" expression moving to a predetermined conclusion, then it does improve faith.[5]

When we're up against it, we'll try almost anything, like the father in the New Testament story who is desperate for help for his epileptic son. He cries out to Jesus, "I believe, help my unbelief!"[6] He was at the edge between hope and despair, between believing that help is available and, at the same time, disbelieving. Somehow in this obscure transaction, a true prayer is born.

Is help available when I need it? It's not a comfortable question for religious liberals. We talk as if self-sufficiency were the ideal. Self-confidence, self-esteem, self-determination—the virtues of the strong and the successful—are proud words in our vocabulary. We think that we shouldn't need help. In the face of adversity we tend to think that we ought to be stoic, our heads "bloody but unbowed." We denigrate spiritual "helps" as crutches for the crippled. But I side with Emily Dickinson; "I like a look of agony," she said, because that's something you can't fake. It is authentic, and therefore holds at least the possibility of new life. I've been spiritually crippled by no more than a head cold! But as the young woman I saw in the hospital reminded me, I also know that spiritual strength can grow when we acknowledge our weaknesses and share this awareness freely.

Beyond Self-Sufficiency

Faith breeds solidarity. Thus, to ask about the availability of help to myself is to be reminded of the need of others for my help. Yes, we help create that in which we believe. So I want to help and encourage the writer of a letter that I received recently:

> Last month, I had need for special emotional help. At an earlier time in my life, I might have had a small New Testament tucked in my purse. Or, if I were Catholic, maybe I would have had a rosary. As I now deepen my commitment to Unitarian Universalism, I became aware that at a time of need for support, I did not have a symbol of my faith to hold to my bosom.

She rebukes religious liberalism's spirit of self-sufficiency; I feel sympathy, but I also feel the sting. To deny your neediness when you need "special emotional help," is to be alienated from your own feelings, a needless and finally destructive form of self-denial. The young woman's letter went on to ask for more interpretation of Unitarian Universalist symbols, such as the flaming chalice.

The flaming chalice is a lamp, a symbol of service. It was adopted as a symbol by the Unitarian Service Committee in the 1940s, when it was working in Czechoslovakia to save refugees from Nazism. Some trace the flaming chalice symbol to Jan Hus, the Czech church reformer who was dishonestly trapped by authorities of the Roman Catholic church and was burned at the stake in 1405. One of Hus's heresies was to protest against the withholding of the communion chalice from the laity. Only the priests drank from the cup of "transubstantiated" wine, lest (they said) a clumsy layperson spill "the blood of Christ." To Hus, the cup of wine had become a clerical privilege, contrary to its purpose as a communion of all Christians. His followers first depicted the chalice with a flame, as a sign of his martyrdom and their cause. In stylized form the flaming chalice is also like a cross, a sign of divine compassion for human brokenness and of the power of sacrificial love.

Today the flaming chalice is usually enclosed within a circle, a symbol of unity. Like any powerful symbol, it carries several meanings: the light of truth, the lamp of service, the flame of Spirit, the cup that is shared in self-giving love, the circle within which we are "at one."

Nevertheless, religious liberals remain "puritans" when it comes to symbols, just as they are reticent when it comes to prayers. Our churches are largely unadorned; too often, our religious services are painfully impersonal. Prayers are eschewed, because "who has a right to pray for me?" (Philosopher Paul Weiss once said that the clearest mark of religious sincerity is not to pray for others, but to ask others to pray for us.) Our language may be poetic, but its vagueness often leaves transcendence unnamed; too often talk *about* religion is substituted for primary or personal religious expression. This is, of course, precisely the way some people want it; not infrequently, they veto efforts to provide more spiritually nourishing fare. The phenomenon is understandable, insofar as people seeking to preserve their intellectual independence take offense when others presume to speak for them. This makes it difficult to find a common language, especially in corporate worship. However, with the growing understanding of the symbolic nature of religious language and the importance of symbolism as a vehicle of religious feeling and meaning, this picture has begun to change, in my view for the better.

The Symbolic Language of Religion

Prayer requires the language of faith, and faith requires symbolic language—words or images that point beyond themselves. Symbols are forms into which various meanings can be poured; but like any powerful instrument, they may be abused. What is the difference between a prayer and a magical incantation? Or an icon and an idol? The line is impossible to define precisely. After going to his wife's high Episcopal church on Christmas Eve, Reinhold Niebuhr said, "Even when we come to the Nicene creed I enjoy it. I should not like to commit myself to it in cold blood. Here poetry has been transmuted into dogma—'very God of very God, begotten not made.' I want to raise some questions about that. But why bother? The choir is singing it to an E flat tune by Eyre. The curse has been taken from the dogma."[7] The music carried him over his doubts.

But if expository prose is too exact, symbolic language may be too vague. Although symbols serve our need for spiritual help, our minds may still balk at the "overbelief" they seem to imply. Then we cling to our doubts, for they seem more certain than our wavering beliefs.

Intellectual honesty is akin to spiritual authenticity, for we cannot be spiritually nourished by what we cannot honestly think through and accept. So doubt is not a bad place to start; still, we cannot end there. Our reticence may signify an exaggerated or unrealistic need to be "independent." When we're up against something more difficult than we had anticipated, we learn what the desperate father meant by the prayer: "I believe, help my unbelief!" It is a cry for help and evokes the faith that help is available.

I love the short, precise prayer of Dante Alighieri, the great Italian poet of the thirteenth century:

> Give us this day our daily manna,
> without which in this rough desert,
> they backward go who toil most to go on.

The lines can serve as a mantra, a brief thought for

"centering." A mantra is a meditative device that helps us take possession of ourselves by focusing on what is central to our spiritual being, letting distractions fall away. To paraphrase Arthur Darby Nock's sense of "primitive" religious belief (cited in Chapter 1), we could say: The God who made anxiety also made the mantra to avert panic. The Russian proverb, "Pray to God and row for the shore," need not be understood as denigrating the importance of prayer. A mantra or prayer that seems useless, on a rational level, may enable us to be reasonable on a spiritual level.

A mantra or short prayer that you have made "your own" can be helpful to have in your memory bank, just as a small, silver flaming chalice or other important symbol worn near to your heart could be spiritually helpful. You never know when you may need it—when, some day, you find yourself toiling onward yet losing heart and slipping backward. At one time or another everyone asks: Is help available when I need it? It's good to be able to say: Yes, I can hold this symbol of wholeness to my bosom—and I can unburden myself, take possession of myself, reappropriate my spiritual energy.

Where We Find Ourselves

The word "manna" signifies food not for the body but for the spirit, something elusive and undefinable, like life itself. The story of the children of Israel being without food in their wilderness wanderings but miraculously fed on "manna from heaven" is told in Exodus 16. Attempts to find naturalistic explanations for such myths are misplaced, for a miracle story is a "teaching story." The story teaches: Do not imagine that your life depends only on your own efforts. Like the flaming chalice, manna is a symbol. It points beyond itself to a source of spiritual nourishment that is always and everywhere at hand, and it invites us to actively appropriate it. It points not so much to what we find within us as to what we find ourselves within: the reality within that we come to ourselves.

A mantra, a symbol, or a deep meditation induces something in us, gives birth to something in us, draws us into participation in the spiritual reality that encompasses us. It is hard to talk about "it" because it's not an "it," an object, something you can observe, define, or analyze. For it is not "out there" to be observed, defined, or analyzed; *it* is that within which we find ourselves. It is that which gives us to ourselves. It engenders in us the new consciousness that I call newmindedness.

Jesus of Nazareth spoke about "the kingdom of God," a symbolic expression for the one spiritual reality on which everything else depends. He invited his listeners to appropriate it; some found the invitation irresistible, and others found it offensive. As a result the Gospels record a series of conflicts, deepening in bitterness, that marked his ministry and apparently led him to "go up to Jerusalem" for a decisive answer. He told "parables of the kingdom," presumably to make perfectly clear what he meant. But the parables remain notoriously obscure, because (like all poetic language) they work by indirection. ("Tell all the truth / But tell it slant," Emily Dickinson recommended.) The kingdom of God—a phrase we might modernize to "the community of God"—is not something you can see. It is something that enables you to see. It is not something you hear, but something that enables you to hear.

The reality of this realm or community of God seems to depend on your being inside it already. It is not about what God created "in the beginning," but what is being created here and now. It is not about what God requires you to do, either to "set things right" or to justify yourself; it is about the potent goodness "in the midst" of you already, waiting to be grasped. It's a participatory experience or nothing. Thus the famous passage:

Being asked by the Pharisees when the kingdom of God was coming, he answered them, "The kingdom of God is not coming with signs to be observed; nor will they say, 'Lo, here it is!' or 'There!' for behold, the kingdom of God is in the midst of you." (Luke 17 : 20–21; Revised Standard Version)

The better-known King James Version translates the key phrase, "the kingdom of God is within you." This translation is not wrong, but it lends itself to a purely individualistic interpretation, a spirituality of "inwardness" rather than a prophetic vision and an active response. What the passage asks for is a transformation of consciousness, in effect saying: "You keep looking around you for it, but you are within it already—would you but awaken to it!" No wonder we have a hard time grasping it. It would be perfectly clear had we but "ears to hear." Through such teasing, challenging, and "off-putting" suggestions, newmindedness is evoked.

Metanoia

The first words Jesus utters in our oldest source, the Gospel of Mark, are these: "The time is fulfilled, and the kingdom of God is at hand; repent and believe in the gospel." (Mark 1 : 15) There are two key phrases here. The New Testament scholar of a generation ago, Joel Henry Cadbury, suggested translating the first phrase, "The kingdom of God is available."[8] "At hand" literally means "within your grasp," hence available. Cadbury's rendering suggests that you cannot passively sit back and wait; you must actively lay hold of this spiritual energy. You must appropriate it. The bold and the importunate, not the polite and proper, are the "winners" in the gospel story. The community of God calls for your participation. It calls forth your affirmation.

Faith—believing in, not believing that—energizes us. I am suggesting that we translate the second phrase:

"Be newminded—energized and renewed—by this good news."9 The New Testament Greek word used here is *metanoia*, literally meaning a change of mind. *Metanoia* is usually translated "repent," a word that has taken on moralistic and threatening overtones. But even "re-pent" has the literal meaning of "re-think." This was the central thrust of Jesus' message: think again. Thus the familiar formula: "You have heard that it was said . . . , but I say unto you. . . ." Rethink everything.

His call to newmindedness challenges habitual patterns of behavior and does so at a level that, in all the generations since his time, we have never been able to catch up, let alone surpass. Loving those who love you is "doin' what comes naturally"; it is characteristic human behavior. It is contractual ("You scratch my back, and I'll scratch yours"), not covenantal. To create a new condition of human existence life requires radically more, a transformation born of absolute good will: "You have heard that it was said, 'You shall love your neighbor and hate your enemy.' But I say to you, Love your enemies and pray for those who persecute you." (Matthew 5 : 43–44)

Sometimes it is said that Jesus rejected the "harsh God" of the Old Testament. I read him differently. What he rejects is the hardening of our understanding of divine intent into "the Law." If God's will is as hard and fast as "the letter of the Law," the legalistic mind says, then we must be no less hard and fast in *our* will and *our* laws. No, Jesus insists, the community of God is one in which love transforms and renews the human will; love does not abrogate the moral law, but enables it to be fulfilled.[10]

Prophetic Vision

In the mythic imagination of the Old Testament, Yahweh, the God of Israel, is so human that sometimes even God must repent and be newminded. That is, God thinks again and changes "his" mind. In some stories God relents from an awful punishment "he" was on the verge of executing. This primitive anthropomorphism has been called unworthy of the modern mind and its supposedly advanced moral sensibilities. But just this capacity for feeling and change marks the astonishing "humanity of God" in the Hebraic imagination. Without it we would not have all those "Bible stories" from which we never cease mining new meanings. They are childlike and yet highly sophisticated. They tell of a God you can appeal to, a God whose wrath might be turned to mercy.

The liberal Protestant minister Harry Emerson Fosdick said that prayer does not change God, but changes us; but this "liberal" view negates what remains lively to the religious imagination, namely God's humanity. Adult faith is a second naiveté, a becoming again like a child. Jesus does not teach new values or beliefs. He was a latter-day prophet among

Jews who revivified the religious imagination by his radical call to newmindedness.

Christian piety has so often claimed that Jesus was thoroughly "original" in his teaching that his true genius, the creative transformation of Hebraic faith, has been obscured. His "new wine" may require "new wineskins," but it is still wine. In fact, the idea of God as a God of love, forgiveness, and compassion was not first asserted by Jesus. Rather, he adopted and radicalized the message of the earlier prophets of Israel in this regard. The community of God that they foretold, when the Law would be written in the human heart (see Jeremiah 31 : 31), he put in the eschatological present. The time is *now*, he said, to fulfill "the word of the Lord" written in the book of Isaiah:

> Is not this the fast that I choose: to loose the bonds of wickedness, to undo the thongs of the yoke, to let the oppressed go free, and to break every yoke? Is it not to share your bread with the hungry, and bring the homeless poor into your house; when you see the naked, to cover [them], and not to hide yourself from your own flesh? . . . Then you shall call, and the Lord will answer: you shall cry, and he will say, Here am I. (Isaiah 58 : 6, 7, 9; Revised Standard Version)

Such is the compassionate love of God, alike for the ancient prophets and for a latter-day prophet of Nazareth. It is not "unconditional love" (as has often been asserted), but a love conditional upon our response. God responds to us in our time of need, when we respond to the need of others, when our deeds fulfill the covenant of justice and mercy.

From this prophetic vision, an authentic and liberating faith is born: Our needs are answered in answering the needs of others. This is the spiritual reality within which we live. Be newminded. The good news is that the community of God is available. You *can* get there from here!

Asking for Help

Once I lived near the far end of the Marblehead (Massachusetts) peninsula, a town crowded with antique houses. The streets are crooked because, it is said, they were originally laid out by cows. People trying to find their way to the neighboring towns of Salem and Lynn would often stop and ask for directions. But that took time, so we'd give them the short answer: "You can't get there from here." Wonderful, the consternation on those faces! But then we'd repent and start the explanation: "Well, first you turn around. . . . " You *can* get there from here.

Is help available when we need it? Yes, it is as close at hand as the community of God. It is gathered like manna in the wilderness and partaken in friendship. It is available:

- when we pause long enough from our toils "to go on," to meditate and to receive, to rethink and even turn around;

- when, being distraught, we cry, "Help my unbelief," and in our very cry, grasp belief;

- when, after being "beside ourselves" with anxiety or grief, we find ourselves within a vastly larger community of caring than we had known;

- when we become centered selves;

- when we enjoy the joy of a child, or any other gift powerful enough to dislodge our self-centered self-concern;

- when we take a symbol of faith and hold it to our bosom—perhaps a flaming chalice as an image of self-giving love within the circle of wholeness;

- when we pray—perhaps for no other gift than to be in the presence of One who will answer, "Here am I."

Emily Dickinson liked "a look of agony" because it does not lie. We are often off-centered, distended, agonized. We seek, then, a sacred wholeness. It encompasses us and is forever newly available to us. Be newminded, for the community of God is at hand!

7

The Dedicated Community

Is religious community a religious necessity?

This ministry we've been entrusted with, God help us if we think it's just ours. We got the chairs, the tables, the building. But we got to remember: We caught a moving train. . . . Malcolm, Martin, Fred Douglass, Mary McLeod Bethune. We have to know these lives. We have to consider what it means if they're really available to us, *really* available to us. . . . There's something about a sense of aloneness that saps your strength. But there's something about togetherness that lets you keep going. And so if there are ancestors who can accompany us, I say reach for them. Because our work isn't going to get any easier.

Johnny Ray Youngblood[1]

Do not separate yourself from the community.

Hillel the Elder (c. 60 BCE–c. 10 CE)

People often say, "I'm a religious person, in my own private way, but I have no use for organized religion." Then they may tell how the nuns rapped their knuckles when they were young, or the preacher in the fundamentalist church of their upbringing was "on the take," or some other horrendous story. Just as often, however, people who are wary of organized religion have had little or no consistent experience of actual religious communities. Perhaps they read something about the crusades in the Middle Ages or the Salem witch trials, and this serves to justify their keeping religious commitments at arm's length thereafter. Churches, it seems, generate suspicion as often as trust.

One man even overcame his misgivings by saying he joined my church because he "didn't believe in organized religion." He meant it seriously, thinking we were utterly different. Hearing this story, those who know churches from within laugh. They know how our volunteerism makes it a constant struggle to "get organized."

Ambivalence Toward Institutional Religion

Speaking to a group of church school children, Brooks Walker, a ministerial colleague of mine, referred to "hypocrites." A hypocrite he defined as someone who says one thing and does another, adding the rhetorical question, "That's pretty ridiculous, isn't it?"

"Yes," a young girl piped up, "unless you happen to

be a hypocrite."

The ambivalence commonly felt about religious institutions is rooted in ambivalence about "religious" people generally. Those who pride themselves on their spirituality or moral goodness are often unbearably self-righteous; lacking a sense of humor about themselves or others, they make us ill at ease. Often, too, we see on closer inspection that they have feet of clay. That is why pride has often been named *the* original sin; and certainly of all forms of pride, spiritual pride is the most unbearable. The myth of Satan tells the tale: Satan took being a God-like angel so seriously that he fell, as G. K. Chesterton put it, of his own gravity.[2] My mother used to say: "Pride goeth before a fall."

There are no myths; there are only versions. Shakespeare makes the implausible seem entirely plausible in his strange cross between tragedy and comedy, *Measure for Measure*. It is a morality play, a variation on the fallen angel story. Angelo, the harsh, puritanical, would-be ruler of Vienna, meets Isabella, the beautiful, passionate would-be nun. We are not surprised when he falls in love and uses the vilest methods in an attempt to seduce her, all the while maintaining his righteousness. The greater the moral pretension, the more blatant the hypocrisy. When irony runs so deep, we need to laugh; indeed, sometimes divine laughter is the only cure. Isabella finally cries out:

But man, proud man,
Drest in a little brief authority,
Most ignorant of what he's most assur'd
(His glassy essence), like an angry ape,
Plays such fantastic tricks before high heaven
As make the angels weep; who, with our spleens,
Would all themselves laugh mortal.[3]

Although keenly aware of the ambiguities of moral protest, I try to listen patiently to scandalized innocents, those for whom the religious community is never good enough. After all, they are right. Still, I can't bring myself to play the righteous Pharisee and say, "Thank goodness *our* church is not like all the others!" At best, I respond: "For a religious person, being part of an actual religious community is inescapable. I hope you will find our church a community that, in spite of its flaws, is dedicated both to your spiritual freedom and to a goodness and a truth that are beyond itself."

The Inescapability of Community

In tradition-bound and communal cultures, no one would be surprised at the statement that religious community is inescapable; in our highly individualistic culture, the idea meets instant resistance.[4] In fact Americans escape institutional religious commitments all the time. However, in both sociological and theological terms, our humanity is morally inconceivable without our being in community. Community is humanly inescapable for all the reasons cited by the noted English political philosopher, Isaiah Berlin, in his book, *Against the Stream*:

> Only if a person truly belongs to a community, naturally and unselfconsciously, can one enter into the living stream and lead a full, creative, spontaneous life, at home in the world and at one with self and one's fellows, enjoying a recognized status, and thereby acquiring a vision of life . . . free from the crippling wounds inflicted by the real or imaginary superiority of others.

To become fully human in isolation from community is developmentally inconceivable. No infant survives and thrives without the fundamental community of a family, including at least the biological or adoptive parents, even if it is a "broken home." Neither do families thrive without the support of the social communities that surround them.

This is only to describe the fact that we are inescapably social beings. It does not explain why religious community is inescapable. At one level, of course, religious community is entirely escapable. We must voluntarily choose it, or it is not "ours." To take personal responsibility for our social commitments is to act out of our creative freedom. The religious community stands for the centrality of community in human life both symbolically and actually. As symbol, it represents our "being in community"; as actuality, it serves the practical needs and well-being of all basic forms of human community—the family, the political community, and the voluntary association. Paul Tillich spoke of faith as ultimate concern, that is, the dimension of ultimacy that is expressed through our various proximate concerns. In this sense, religious community is the ultimate concern that underlies our various proximate concerns for community; church is both a theological and a sociological category.

Because we find it so difficult to think of the church as a theological concept, words of explanation are in order. To speak of something as inescapable, as I have in this and other contexts, is to say it is fundamental to our being. It is to speak theologically. For instance, Forrester Church, minister of the Unitarian Church of All Souls in New York City, defines religion as "our human response to the dual reality of being alive and having to die." Awakening to first realities, the inescapability of living and dying, questions of ultimate concern become inescapable.[5] How we respond to the fundamental "inescapabilities" of existence is a matter of our free will; and yet, to respond in some way is unavoidable. We are "fated to be free," in James Luther Adams's phrase.

Religious Community as a Religious Issue

How we live in community is not just a practical or political or moral question. It is a spiritual question, for it involves the uses and abuses of our freedom in the face of our inescapably social nature. Becoming conscious of these processes and taking responsibility for them, we both consent to and dissent from our communities. The religious community symbolizes the spiritual dimension of our social existence and actively works to uphold spiritual and moral values within both itself and the other forms of community.

This is why a theology is incomplete without what is traditionally called a doctrine of the church. Each of us must ask and decide: Is religious community *religiously* important to me? Can I be authentically religious without it? Or can I take it or leave it, depending on my personal wish or whim? "I'm not a joiner," many say; some even think that churches are an encumbrance to a truly spiritual life. We may think of Buddhists as solitary meditators, but in fact Buddhists are part of a historical tradition and community; the Buddha himself taught his followers to "take refuge in the *sangha*," the community of faith. A doctrine of the church recognizes that religious community is not an optional luxury but a necessity of authentic religious faith.

When the ancient Jewish teacher, Hillel the Elder, warned against separating ourselves from the community, he was reminding us to be dedicated to something larger than ourselves. He did not mean, of course, just anything "larger than ourselves," but that community which applies the test of ultimacy to all things, including itself. An authentic, dedicated community is a self-critical community. It is rooted in a tradition against which it measures itself. It establishes standards with which it judges its own practices. It is not subjected to the whims of any individual who claims direct inspiration by the Spirit; John Buehrens cites the principle enunciated by the influential Unitarian minister of the nineteenth century, Henry Whitney Bellows: "The Holy Spirit speaks most reliably through the group." Above all, it is dedicated to a transcendent ideal, by which it knows how far it succeeds or misses the mark. The ideal cannot be defined in simple terms; it can only be spoken of symbolically, as, for instance, "the community of God."

As an alternative to the term "church," I often use the term "faith community" or "religious community." In ecumenical gatherings, especially around common social concerns, other non-particularist terms have come into use: "people of faith" and "covenant people." Here I will use yet another term, one I learned from the philosopher Paul Weiss: the dedicated community.[6]

Dedicated to what? The question calls for a multifaceted answer, and sometimes the best way to give such an answer is to tell a story about it. Two intertwined stories follow.

Communal Passages

The Jewish feast of Passover falls during the same season as the Christian Holy Week, culminating in Good Friday and Easter. Their coincidence is not, of course, coincidental, for the Christian story is built upon the Jewish story. (There are no myths; there are only versions.) Both are crisis stories, and the passages through crisis they relate mark the beginnings of new communities of faith, the Jewish and the Christian— communities fatefully intertwined down to this day. These stories cannot be reduced to a formula; they resist rational explanation. They contain a mystery that can only be understood by placing ourselves within the stories being told; a sacred story is always one we are *in*.

Passover tells of the passage over the homes of the Israelites in Egypt by the Angel of Death—a frightful prelude to the people's passage through the Red Sea, to the freedom of their self-determination as a community.[7] Good Friday tells a similar story: Jesus was abandoned, even by his friends, to the Romans and to death, a ghastly execution on a cross. The Christian story is another frightful prelude to another people's passage, to freedom from the dominating power of death over our lives.

I cannot untangle the many strands of meaning in such stories; the patterns, like life itself, are obscure. I can only observe and comment on a few elements of them, as historical stories of the birth of a new community and as existential stories of personal rebirth. Both tell of a time of testing, and of the bond felt by those who experience the testing.

The founding of a religious community seems to depend on its passage through a soul-deep trial; a person's entrance into the community follows a parallel course. There are not only successes; there are also failures. Conscience convicts us of careless disregard— our failure to take serious commitments seriously. Sometimes it convicts us of outright betrayal—our failure to count the costs of friendship. But when our hearts reassert themselves, new, unbounded commitments and friendships are born.

For those who identify with the Jewish Passover story or the Christian Passion story, these stories evoke the movement from obliviousness to awakening, from betrayal to repentance, or from brokenness to wholeness. They become, then, moments of fresh self-recognition and commitment. That is when religious community by whatever name—the church, the dedicated community, the covenant people—becomes personally inescapable. These experiences shatter our complacency and our pride, the things that cause us to separate ourselves from the community.

The Interdependence of Community and Person

The dedicated community matters. It matters as deeply as anything in this world, I believe, for sustaining and renewing those spiritual realities that make and keep human life human. We seek out and affiliate with a religious community when we remember these realities and seek to renew them. Religious communities, no less than any other kind, are not above criticism. The dedicated community invites us to criticize and enlarge our social and political communities, but neither does it exempt itself from criticism and *re*-formation. It does so in the name of a greater reality, the community of God.

In sum we may say that the dedicated community matters in relation to three inescapabilities of human life:

- our need for a deeply shared communal identity,
- our need to be enlisted in ends beyond ourselves, and
- our need for help when we are stuck in self-defeat.

In these fundamental respects, the dedicated community opens a sacred space in our lives. It becomes a place fit, in A. Powell Davies' phrase, "to grow a soul." The dedicated community holds common meanings and values that support the freedom and dignity of each person. It enables us to act for a more just, compassionate, and peaceful social order. It helps us overcome the isolation, the unreliability, and the encroaching darkness of our own hearts.

Laurel Hallman, minister of the First Unitarian Church of Dallas, Texas, tells the story of a dour, reclusive Scotsman who was not in church for many Sundays. His Presbyterian pastor went to visit him in his humble cottage. When the pastor knocked, the Scotsman opened the door and, without a word, motioned the pastor inside. The man indicated a rocking chair in front of the coal fire for the pastor. He drew up another chair for himself. In silence, the two men sat and watched the burning coals. After a time the pastor stood up, took the fire tongs and put one of the glowing coals to the side of the hearth. He sat down again and began to rock. Both men watched the lone coal as it grew ashen and cold. After a time the pastor again took the tongs, picked up the dead coal, and put it back in the fire. Then he sat down and both men watched as once again it burned brightly with the rest. Without a word the pastor left. The next week the old Scotsman was in church and never missed a Sunday from that time forward.

The first moral of this story is obvious. *Each soul, like each coal in the fireplace, needs the community that keeps it alive*. It works the other way around, as well, for the pastor represents a community that missed the Scotsman and felt deprived of his unique gifts. So we can also say: *Each soul, like a coal, helps build the community that warms and sustains us all*. This second moral is equally important. In the symmetry of the moral covenant, we can say: Every soul needs its community, but equally, every community needs the souls who sustain it. In the dedicated community we are all agents of a shared ministry to one another and to the world beyond us.

(Actually, the story is too perfect. *Never* missed a Sunday thereafter? That's bad practice. Homer Jack, I'm told, once told his parishioners that sometimes they would get more spiritual nourishment from a walk in the woods than from attending church. Yes, the woods are also one of our sacred communities.)

Stories Within Stories

A religion without a story to tell, a history to recite, is dead. In one of her several careers, my wife, Barbara Kres Beach, was a dancing art educator. She would go barefoot in the marble halls of the Cleveland Museum of Art, leading a band of barefoot boys and girls through the paintings, responding to them in movement.[8] The body has a language that words cannot express. And sometimes, when the language of the body is felt in the muscles and bones, movement evokes insight and gives the body voice.

One day, Barbara was leading a group of 10- and 11-year-olds through their kinesthetic responses. First, they came to El Greco's elongated, stormy-skied "Christ on the Cross with Landscape," and then to Murillo's exultant, cherub-strewn image of Mary, "The Ascension of the Virgin." "What's a virgin, Mrs. Beach?" one child asked. Finally they came to Georges de La Tour's "The Repentant Peter." In the painting an aged Peter stares straight ahead; the cock that crowed stands before him. He clutches his hands together, and tears stream down his cheeks.

Barbara had the children try out the tense gaze and the clutching gesture. "What's happening here?" she asked. A young boy said, "He's squeezing his hands together so tight that the water is coming out of his eyes."

When we forget, the body helps us remember. This is the story behind the painting:

> After a little while the by-standers came up and said to Peter, "Certainly you are also one of them, for your accent betrays you." [He was a Galilean; they, Jerusalemites.] Then he began to invoke a curse on himself and to swear, "I do not know the man." And immediately the cock crowed. And Peter remembered what Jesus had said, "Before the cock crows, you will deny me three times." And he went out and wept bitterly. (Matthew 26 : 73–75; Revised Standard Version)

Barbara and the children came next to an old Dutch masterpiece, Gerhard van Hornhorst's "Samson and Delilah." In the painting Samson's sleeping head lies in Delilah's lap. Delilah gently takes a long lock of Samson's hair in one hand, while the other is poised for a snip. It is a moment poised for treachery. Another young boy's voice piped up: "Finally, a Jewish picture!"

And yet, the themes of the two paintings are not so different: a moment of betrayal, a moment portending a death. Both are images related to the primary and parallel biblical themes, Passover/Exodus and Passion/Easter.

We hear stories within stories, linking personal experience, cultural and religious history, and existence itself, in widening concentric circles. We hear (a) what a young boy said in the art museum, (b) about a seventeenth-century Dutch painting, (c) that interprets a dramatic incident in the Gospels, (d) set within a vast biblical epic. The epic (e) captures a complex interplay of historical and even cosmic forces, experienced as (f) powers that lift us up, cast us down, and sometimes lift us up again. These multiple layers of meaning heighten our consciousness and enrich our understanding of ourselves and "our people." These stories impassion us, sometimes becoming our personal stories and sometimes, the stories of our world-age. They call forth something unaccountable in us, and move us to dedicate ourselves to ends that both join us and transcend us.

So do we become members of a dedicated community. The stories we tell lend weight and direction to our lives. They lighten the darkness in our hearts, they kindle newmindedness. The most powerful stories work a kind of magic, because they catch our consciences, taking us by surprise, and transform our consciousness. In Hamlet's words,

The play's the thing
Wherein I'll catch the conscience of the king.[9]

A Costly Spiritual Heritage

People often ask me how, or why, I became a minister. There are several stories within the story, like the layers of an onion, as there are for any of us who seek to "explain ourselves." But it is the innermost layer that people want to hear about—the personal answer that I am sometimes the most reluctant to give.

This, then, is a story about how my religious conscience was caught. I believe it also helps explain why I, raised a Unitarian, am forever humanizing the Bible and theologizing humanism.

I had heard James Luther Adams speak when I was an Oberlin College undergraduate. He had moved from Meadville Theological School where he taught social ethics to Harvard Divinity School, the year before, and this more than anything else moved me to choose Harvard. Shortly before entering Harvard, I had read Adams's autobiographical essay, "Taking Time Seriously"; a passage caused me physically to shudder:

Nathan Soederblom has remarked that Bach's *St.*

Matthew Passion should be called the Fifth Evangelist. So was Bach for me. One night after singing with the Harvard Glee Club in the *Mass in B Minor* under Serge Koussevitzky at Symphony Hall in Boston, a renewed conviction came over me that here in the mass, beginning with the *Kyrie* and proceeding through the *Crucifixus* to the *Agnus Dei* and *Dona nobis pacem*, all that was essential in the human and the divine was expressed. My love of the music awakened in me a profound sense of gratitude to Bach for having displayed as through a prism and in a way that was irresistible for me, the essence of Christianity.

I realize now that this was only the culmination of my *praeparatio evangelica* [preparation for the Gospel]. For suddenly I wondered if I had a right even to enjoy what Bach had given me. I wondered if I was not a spiritual parasite, one who was willing to trade on the costly spiritual heritage of Christianity, but who was perhaps doing very little to keep that heritage alive. In the language of Kierkegaard, I was forced out of the spectator into the "existential" attitude. This experience was, to be sure, not a new one: It was simply a more decisive one. I could now see what Nietzsche meant when, in speaking of the *Passion* music, he said, "Whoever has wholly forgotten Christianity will hear it there again."[10]

Adams's religious background was very different from my own; he was raised Plymouth Brethren, a full-fledged fundamentalist, and I was a "briar patch" Unitarian. Yet Bach's *St. Matthew Passion* had also worked its magic on me. When I first read Adams's words, I was already set on becoming a Unitarian minister. But I was utterly uncertain what I believed or how to identify the community of faith to which I was dedicated. Adams's story evoked my own growing recognition that I, too, depended on a "costly spiritual heritage," a heritage that was far larger and more complex than I had imagined. But this was the incisive question: Would I contribute to it or only feed off it?

I have called myself a Christian humanist.[11] My spiritual heritage is rooted in the prophets of the Old Testament, who proclaimed that "what the Lord requires" is deeds of justice, steadfast love, faithfulness, uprightness, truth-telling, and peace-making. This heritage was renewed by "the prophet Jesus from Nazareth in Galilee," as the people of his time identified him (Matthew 21 : 11). This latter-day prophet so radicalized his faith tradition that he transformed it. As a result, Jesus mediated the substance of Judaic faith to the gentile world.

Yet he did not do it alone: He depended on a dedicated band he drew to himself like fish in a net. They were led by the same man, Peter, whose painful story of denial—saying no when he should have said yes—

was depicted in the painting by Georges de La Tour. It was a denial first foretold and then painfully remembered, like Adams's story of mixed emotions when he sang the Bach mass, like my story of my complex response to reading Adams.

To be sure, the open-minded, critical, and humanistic legacy of Unitarianism was part of my own "costly spiritual heritage." It was in my bones, even as I rebelled against it. I rebelled against it because it often seemed mindlessly bent on dispossession of our Jewish and Christian inheritance. Dispossession is too thin a gruel to live on. Thus Adams's self-questioning became my own. What, I asked myself, would I contribute to the renewal of my liberal and Christian heritage of prophetic faith?

Remembering Who We Are

The dedicated community is formed, shaken up, and formed anew when we discover our personal story within earlier stories of our heritage. When we permit our story to grow within the embrace of our common story, we strengthen one another. Then we take risks to realize a shared vision of justice and peace that we would never have taken alone.

Yet challenges we did not anticipate, and crises we did not count the cost of, will come. When we betray our commitments, too lightly made; when we abandon friends, too unsteadily loved; when we give way to careless disregard, then we are reminded, conscience-stricken. We remember who we are and cannot not be.

The dedicated community forms and reforms our sense of being a people—a people with work to do. It inspires our dreams and goads us to take courage and act upon them. It rescues us from ourselves—by letting us accept our own imperfections, by lending support when our strength slackens, by offering forgiveness. It accepts our gifts of renewed good will, and gives us to ourselves. Such is the community of God we never quite are, and yet are dedicated to be.

8

Parabolic Vision

Does faith make sense?

The more faithfully you listen to the voice within
you, the better you will hear what is sounding
outside. And only he who listens can speak. Is this
the starting point of the road towards the union of
your two dreams—to be allowed in clarity of mind
to mirror life and in purity of heart to mold it?

Dag Hammarskjold[1]

This is about the stillness in moving things,
In running water, also in the sleep
Of winter seeds, where time to come has tensed
Itself, enciphering a script so fine
Only the hourglass can magnify it, only
The years unfold its sentence from the root.

Howard Nemerov[2]

The lines by Howard Nemerov cited above begin a long
poem and announce its "theme"—

. . . of thought and the defeat
Of thought before its object, where it turns
As from a mirror. . . .

The preceding chapters have similarly been concerned with the existential reality we try to penetrate and make sense of, as well as with the inevitability of thought's defeat when "last things," ultimacies, are at stake. Then the mind turns back upon itself, as from a mirror; although the images are puzzling or paradoxical, something like transcendence is glimpsed. But we do not forget it.

We cannot *not* reflect on transcendence, whatever language of religion or no-religion we adopt; the moral integrity and the spiritual wholeness of our lives depend on it. For many people this affirmation, if it is not nonsense, still is fraught with difficulties. Indeed, justifying it seems to me the hardest step in the religious journey I have traced. Tacitly, we have taken this step at each stage along the way, because each chapter has reflected on some aspect of the inescapability of transcendence and our need for self-transcendence. Although I explicitly address the question of the necessity and the integrity of faith only now, at the end of the journey, it is in a sense the first step, the *first* question to which I answer *yes*.

Why Believe In Anything?

I once gave a sermon, "This I Believe," taking the Edward R. Murrow series of the 1950s with this title as my model. Toward the end I summarized, saying: I believe in the presence of transcendence; I believe in the creative freedom of the human spirit; I believe in the transforming power of love; I believe in the dedicated community of all souls. The pattern reflected in these four affirmations should, by this time, be familiar. To be sure, the preceding chapters have sought to flesh out this bare-bones outline. Perhaps because earlier glimpses of transcendence are so difficult to hold onto in their original clarity, I come back at the end to a prior question: *Why* do I believe in these things? I suppose that all of us, with regard to our own once-settled beliefs, return to this question, occasionally or often. We may even ask it in its most radical form: Why believe in anything at all?

I do not believe what I do on account of tradition or authority; to me, appeals to the authority of a book or a church do not satisfy my need to make my affirmations "my own." Martin Luther understood this when he said, "Everyone must do their own believing and their own dying."[3] Neither do I believe on account of arguments or evidence. If I had rationally convincing arguments or evidence, I could say "this I know" rather than "this I believe." But since our knowing will always be partial and fallible, believing is unavoidable. What, then, is intelligently believable?

A great deal is at stake in the confidence we have in our answer to this question. As it has been said, "If you don't believe in something, you'll fall for anything." It is curious how often people actually do slip over the line from utter skepticism into utter gullibility. In fact, whole cultures are capable of such a radical slippage. Is it hyperbolic to suggest that, in the 1960s, when scientism and radicalism ruled, we believed in *nothing*, whereas in the 1970s we managed to believe in *everything*—any and all of 57 varieties of popular psychology, occult science, and "new age" thought? In religion too, it seems, nature abhors a vacuum.

The question remains: What motivates and validates particular beliefs, or even belief itself?

A Symbol of Transformation

What we believe is neither more nor less than that which enables us to make sense of life. I use the term "making sense" in the ordinary, colloquial way that we may say of an explanation, "That makes sense." We mean more than: This fits my prior understanding of the way things are. We mean: This enables me to make sense of other things, such that they fit together in ways that they did not before. What "makes sense" is the insight or the intuition that what was obscure, paradoxical, or even nonsensical before, becomes intelligible when seen "in this light." It fulfills my need for confidence that life's seeming contradictions can be reconciled, and its seeming absurdities can be overcome. I need this confidence to act with moral courage and steadfast hope.

Why, for instance, would I risk loving someone when I know that the loss of this person and this love will bring me greater pain than I knew before? Consider the pathos underlying the epitaph on the tombstone of an infant in an old Puritan graveyard:

> I wonder what I was begun for,
> Seeing I am so soon done for?

Why be committed to anyone or anything, when disappointment, disillusionment, or betrayal *may* be the bitter result? To answer these questions requires of us a certain faith, insight, or passion—something that carries us over the chasm of pain and dread. How this happens remains difficult to explain.

We make sense of things by insight, by casting them in a new light, or sometimes, like King Oedipus, by a shock of recognition. Then, what had seemed meaningless becomes profoundly meaningful. Religious meaning, at least, seems to require of us a transformation. If religion is centrally concerned with fulfillment (wholeness, salvation, justification, and at-oneness are expressions of it) then, I am saying, we must be transformed on the way to fulfillment. Parabolic vision is a symbol of transformation.

Belief is purposeful. Following St. Anselm's insight, I have said that we believe purposefully: I believe in order that I may understand. Hence the question: Does faith make sense? Does it enable me to understand things that, otherwise, would be obscure, baffling, defeating? What is it, then, that troubles my heart and mind, and what affirmations of faith enable me to bear this "trouble" and be a spiritually whole person nevertheless? If yes is the answer, what is the question? The preceding chapters have marched through many variations on this theme. This concluding chapter brings the discussion back to the place where it began, the personal level of experience and reflection. Like a stone thrown in the air, it comes back to earth, but in a new place.

Two Examples

To clarify what I mean by "parabolic vision," consider two examples, lines by the English poet and artist, William Blake, and the brief account of a religious experience by Ann Maginnis, a layperson in the church I serve as minister.

> To see the World in a Grain of Sand,
>   And a Heaven in a Wild Flower,
> Hold Infinity in the palm of your hand,
>   And Eternity in an hour.

These opening lines of Blake's "Auguries of Innocence" have an instant, intuitive appeal. They are symmetrical: He instructs us to hold to what is tiny, a grain of sand, in order to see what is *infinite*, "the World." And he instructs us to attend to what quickly passes, a wild flower, in order to see what is *eternal*, "a Heaven." Blake is not so much describing something as evoking something—a transformation of consciousness that points to its fulfillment. "Infinity" and "Eternity" lie beyond our ordinary experience but are implicit within space and time. Infinity fulfills the potentiality of space, and eternity fulfills the potentiality of time. We do not reach these "fulfillments" by indefinite extension—imagining endless space or endless time—but by imaginative transformations. The poem concludes:

> God appears, and God is Light,
>> To those poor souls who dwell in Night;
> But does a Human Form display
>> To those who dwell in realms of Day.

"Light" is a primary symbol of God to "those poor souls" who cannot see, for it transforms the "Night"; those fortunate enough to "dwell in realms of Day," are fulfilled already, for their own "Human Form" becomes a primary symbol of God. Blake is a poet of parabolic vision *par excellence*.

All of us, I think, dwell in both of Blake's symbolic places, Night and Day, at various times in our lives. We seek both *transformation* and *fulfillment*, the two primary directives of the religious quest. Consider the words of Ann Maginnis, spoken in a church service, about her experience while observing the birds at her window feeder:

> The design and texture of the feathers is a fine tapestry. What elaborate craftsmanship was lavished on these common birds. And in this act of noticing, crusty coverings are lifted from me and I feel a slipping sensation along my nerves that gives the air hands, and I am robed in this simple certainty: that I am part of something larger than myself and that my actions have meaning; I can either preserve or I can destroy.

She begins with simple attentiveness and ends with personal confidence and moral commitment; thus her words become a parable bearing a personal meaning that is much greater than the brief experience that occasioned it. An "outer" experience of beauty becomes an "inner" experience of wonder. Her sense that the boundaries between self and world were dissolved, in that moment, indicate what I've called *transformation*. What to others might have been only an aesthetic experience became for her a spiritual and a moral experience. Thus she speaks of a sense of spiritual *fulfillment*: "I am robed in this simple certainty—the certainty that she is part of, and at one with, a larger whole. Finally, she affirms a moral meaning of the experience: "my actions have meaning," either to preserve or to destroy life. Feeding the birds exemplifies a commitment to preserve life. The parabolic vision is not only seen or felt, it is enacted.

It is notable that both William Blake's and Ann Maginnis's parables begin with acts of attentiveness. There is a long tradition of "contemplative prayer," prayer that begins with and stays with the contemplation of one "simple" thing. In Simone Weil's words, "Attention is an acceptable form of prayer."[4] "Listen" was one of Jesus' repetitive watchwords; the parable of the sower begins, "Listen! A sower went out to sow." After he has told the parable, the disciples ask Jesus to interpret its meaning; he replies, with apparent indignation, "Do you not understand this parable? How then will you understand all the parables?" (See Mark 4 : 3-13.) "The sower" is a parable of parables—of "parabolic vision" itself. It says: Without attentiveness to what is happening around us, and an awakening to its ultimate import, no other religious messages or stories will make sense.

Jesus the Parable Teller

Mark's Gospel goes on to say that Jesus "did not speak to them without a parable" (4 : 34), a notion that may surprise us because it suggests that *all* of his utterances were parabolic. We think of "the parables of

Jesus" as stories, told in the manner of a preacher who wishes to make his point vivid and memorable. But when we see that Mark considered this parabolic language a kind of esoteric language, which only "insiders" could truly understand, we recognize that something is being said about the form of Jesus' message, or indeed, about the content of his message as a whole. "The kingdom of God" that Jesus proclaimed is not a place or a time, but a symbolic representation of transcendence; it is paradoxically both present and yet to come—both "fulfilled in your hearing" (Luke 4 : 21) and yet to be fulfilled in your deeds.

Jesus was a thoroughgoing exponent of parabolic vision. Several times, in several ways, he instructs his listeners to forgive in order that they may be forgiven. It seems, at first blush, like an oddly self-serving reason for forgiving, that is, for releasing others from their moral debts to us. But it also entails the insight that we forgive not from a position of moral superiority, but rather of equality, when we recognize that we, too, need forgiveness. Thus forgiving is a purposeful form of action, one that fulfills "the moral covenant": our own spiritual fulfillment depends on the absolute good will of seeking the fulfillment of others. Just this is the meaning of love. When I love you, your happiness becomes mine, your life becomes a parable—a likeness—of my life.

The life of Jesus the parable-teller became, from the very rise of Christianity, a central parable of faith. The

Easter story is a story of transformation and fulfillment. It transcends and yet enables moral and spiritual self-understanding. To those persons like myself for whom Jesus of Nazareth is a prophetic and a pioneering figure of faith, Easter remains a central holy day. It is rooted in ideas of spiritual death and rebirth that predate Christianity, but because it is bound up with the memory of a historical person and has been carried forward by a historical community, Easter cannot be reduced to a festival of the spring equinox. We live as inescapably in history as we do in nature. But neither can Easter be viewed in purely historical terms, as a factual report of past events. It will mean less than nothing if we are oblivious to present Easter experiences.

Resurrection

The story of Jesus' resurrection is a mythic response to the memory of his ministry of teaching and healing, a story abruptly terminated by his execution on a cross.[5] To those who had followed him, his crucifixion must have been a frightful, heart-rending experience. His impact on them during his life was incalculable; now, suddenly, he was gone. Only if he lives on among us, they concluded, did he not live and die in vain. They felt: In our weakness and "little faith" we abandoned him, but he did not abandon us. Thus his teaching of forgiveness took on transforming significance: nevertheless, you are accepted. The Easter story became a teaching story in the early church. When the women come to anoint Jesus' body in the tomb, they are asked by the angels who are there, "Why do you seek the living among the dead?" (Luke 24 : 5) The question is parabolic: The spirit of this man is not found in the tomb of your despair and grief; he goes before you, into Galilee and beyond. The story's meaning is contemporaneous.

We can reappropriate this language of faith as we begin to recognize its symbolic character. I do not call the Easter story a myth to debunk and jettison it, but to release its power. Powerful myths are like atoms; they must be broken—recognized as symbolic rather than literal stories—in order to release their energy. When we see in them the stories of our own lives, we discover their transforming power.

"Resurrection" is a powerful symbol in human consciousness. Recently, a letter came to my wife and me from a young woman whom we had met during a visit to the Unitarian churches in Romania. She is single, a teacher, and an avid reader; she lives with a congenital physical impairment. I quote from her letter here:

> I'm still not living the best period of my life, and prospects are even darker. Yet, I'm still more cheerful than most people around me. Sometimes I'm afraid their gloom might be a catching disease. Exhaustion seems to be as infinite as time itself. But hopefully I'll manage, as I have done so far. And I promise I won't complain when we see

each other. (It'll be great!) And now, close to Easter, let me thank you again for your repeated help in my emotional, spiritual resurrection. I wish your kindness to be a kind of boomerang returning to you and your family a hundredfold. Love, E.

"Resurrection" signifies her sense of absolute hope in the midst of her personal difficulties, a transforming power. Such a spiritual experience does not come "out of the blue," as a disembodied belief. Her words suggest, rather, that it is mediated from person to person; it elicits promises ("I won't complain") and promises joy ("It'll be great!") It seems to arise most powerfully when we make our lives into parables of other lives, telling the story of our love in words and deeds. It makes of "kindness," once received, "a kind of boomerang."

Pattern, Parable, Parabola

Making sense of life is more than an intellectual project. It draws together the four levels of consciousness that have been a recurrent theme in this book: awakening, understanding, deciding, and acting. The movement I have described begins with awareness, often felt as an awakening to something to which we had been oblivious. "And Jacob awakened out of his sleep, and he said, Surely the Lord is in this place, and I knew it not!" (Genesis 28 : 16; King James Version) Awareness, then, focuses our intellectual questioning—the drive to understand—by analyzing, conceptualizing, and relating. But it is not enough to understand life; we must also make judgments of meaning and value. There are many possibilities; to decide is to cut off all but one. Nevertheless, the choice is not arbitrary, because it is qualified by all that has gone before it. As awareness qualifies our understandings, suffusing them with feeling, understanding qualifies our judgments, rendering them reasonable. Thus consciousness is heightened as we move from awareness to understanding, and from understanding to decision. The aim of the process—implicit from the start and drawing us toward the conclusion—is to appropriate our capacities to act purposefully and to good effect. The entire movement toward heightened conscious intentionality enables us, in the final stage, to act responsibly for the common good.

Only such a fully conceived faith makes sense. For faith is an unaccountable affirmation: the *yes* of intuitive feeling, of illuminating insight, of reasoned decision, of ultimate commitment. As this cumulative process has borne this fruit in many good lives we see about us, so can it in our lives.

I picture these themes in the pattern of a parabola. Like the curved line that is traced by a stone thrown in the air, the upward trajectory mirrors the way downward. Unless the stone is thrown straight up (and even this, of course, is an illusion on a moving earth), it comes down in a different place. Parabolic vision is intended, then, as a metaphor for the entire cycle of "first questions." It is also a metaphor for the pattern of our lives.

The words, parable and parabola, both derive from the Greek, *parabole*, meaning literally "to throw beside." The ancient Greeks were probably the first to give precise definition to a parabola: a curved line that approaches a plane and then sails off again. (To be precise: Any point on the curve, measured perpendicular to the plane, is equidistant between the plane and a focal point.) Carried far enough, the two ends of a parabolic curve become ever more nearly parallel, but never quite get there. The line sails into infinity. Perhaps that is why I have always thought of it as an image of eternity. Pythagoras held that the universe is made not of earth, air, fire and water, but of number. Perhaps he was right!

A parable is a comparison of two things that may seem disparate but throw new light on each other. Religiously significant parables illuminate what is mysterious—things that are obscure and are sources of wonder.

We dwell within mystery. Of some of the most important things in life we can only say, "Time will tell." Therefore we must live by faith. Something fundamental to our being and essential to our well-being is obscure, hidden from our direct apprehension—something like a seed in which "time to come has tensed itself, enciphering a script . . . " (Howard Nemerov).

Thus, understanding requires a kind of double vision that is able, for instance, to see "the stillness in moving things." It requires a recognition that we see, yet do not see. We have an inkling of the truth, yet we do not see steadily enough or far enough to still the restlessness of our hearts. We want more. Surely, we reflect, others have seen further than we into the meaning and the truth of things, and we can follow their lead. Arthur Darby Nock once told of the Igulik Eskimo who said, "Our shamen can see farther into the snows than you or I can see. We trust them, for otherwise the animals would disappear and we would die." Prophetic visionaries in many traditions have cast up luminous symbols to dispel the mystery. It is this casting up of symbols that I call parabolic vision. Sacred symbols illumine the way before us, inviting us to step into the light.

Transformation and Fulfillment

The entry from *Markings* cited at the head of this chapter reflects Dag Hammarskjold's quest for spiritual fulfillment; he calls it "the union of your two dreams." He, too, is concerned with the close fit between inner and outer meanings. He, too, begins with the self-discipline of attentiveness: "And only those who listen can speak." He, too, seeks transformation for the sake of fulfillment and action. The day's entry, which I have cited *in toto*, does not explain what his two longings were; probably these "dreams" are symbols that bear various specific, personal meanings. The "road towards the union of your two dreams" seems to signify a transformation he seeks on the path toward a longed-for fulfillment. He seeks to "mirror" life with "clarity of mind" and to "mold" it in "purity of heart." In the end, he believes, these pairs of terms (mirroring/clarity of mind, and molding/purity of heart) must be united.

"Markings," in Swedish, is *Wegmaerken*, trail markers. Hammarskjold said that the short entries in his journal were signposts of his life-journey, the record of "my negotiations with myself and with God." When the book was published in 1961, shortly after his death, even close friends of this famous public figure, the Secretary General of the United Nations, were astonished. They had had no inkling of the often anguished, sometimes ecstatic spiritual life that the book disclosed. Some entries record his keen observations on life; others, the pain he felt for the moral disorder of the world. A few, like the following, record intense religious experiences.

A sunny day in March. Within the birch tree's slender shadow on the crust of snow, the freezing stillness of the air is crystallized. Then—all of a sudden—the first blackbird's piercing note of call, a reality outside yourself, the real world. All of a sudden—the Earthly Paradise from which we have been excluded by our knowledge.[6]

The words illustrate Hammarskjold's occasional break-through to a clearer and more powerful reality than he had felt before. He calls it the revelation of "a reality outside yourself, the real world," apparently to accent his feeling that this experience liberated him from a state of psychic self-involvement in which reality and illusion are confused. He is "awakened" by something external, a bird's call. When he says that we are "excluded by our knowledge" from "the Earthly Paradise" (the beauty and enjoyment of nature), clearly he is thinking of the biblical story of Adam and Eve. They were excluded from Paradise when they ate from "the tree of the knowledge of good and evil." That knowledge and maturity should "exile" us from self and world, leaving us to seek to break through a sense of estrangement, is a central paradox of human experience.

The paradox is part of our common experience. For instance, we do not hold children fully responsible for their deeds; we "make allowances" for their behavior. But if we did not hold them responsible *at all*, how would they ever learn responsibility? We constantly live with such ambiguities, sometimes erring on the one side, sometimes on the other. Sometimes, when the trouble seems intractable or especially pernicious, we must try very hard not to give up. We want our children to "grow up," yet not sooner than they can manage.

Does "knowledge," in the sense of consciousness of having done wrong, create sin? The Apostle Paul noted that there is no sin—no willful moral violation—without the consciousness of sin. In this paradoxical sense the law itself creates sin, and the only healthy conscience is a guilty conscience![7] On first tasting ice cream, essayist André Gide is said to have said, "Mmmm, too bad it isn't a sin!"—for then it would be all the more enjoyable. Such are the ambiguities of our moral experience.

The movement from ignorance to knowledge may seem to us unambiguously good. But when ignorance is associated with naiveté or innocence, gaining knowledge loses its goodness; "a little learning" and knowledge without wisdom can be dangerous things. Something is gained, and something else is lost. The burdens of freedom and responsibility are gained; blissful ignorance is lost. We wish we could recapture our children's "dreaming innocence," and yet childishness in an adult is grotesque. "The Fall" into "the knowledge of good and evil" has been called original sin; I prefer to call it "original responsibility," the awareness that making moral decisions is inescapable. Choosing between good and evil is implicit in every choice we make; we cannot not choose. Feeling the weight of moral responsibility, we experience freedom not as a liberation but as a burden.

We long, then, for what has been called "second naiveté," a naiveté that is joyful and "pure in heart" and yet is wiser than childhood's original (or first) naiveté. We long for "songs of innocence" deepened and tempered by our having known "songs of experience" (William Blake). We long for self-transcendence.

Hammarskjold, too, longed for spiritual transformation and fulfillment:

> What I ask for is absurd: that life shall have a meaning. What I strive for is impossible: that my life shall acquire a meaning. I dare not believe, I do not see how I shall ever be able to believe: that I am not alone. [8]

Faith does not "make sense" in the sense of being commonsensical. It is not strictly rational, but neither is it irrational. Far from being smug, it is often deeply troubled by the moral disorder of the world. If faith "makes sense" it will not be because we have reduced our beliefs to what seems reasonable. It will be because our confidence and commitment enable us to affirm what Pascal called "the reasons of the heart," the reasons that transcend mere "reason."

Epilogue

Finally, consider a story of the spirit of life trying to get through to us in spite of immense and painful difficulties. After a hospital visit some years ago, I reflected:

> Elizabeth has broken her hip. In her elderly deafness and near-blindness, her life has become a

burden to be waited out. Also, there is *pain* to be endured, and almost unbroken loneliness. She asks why God does not take her life forthwith; I have no good answer. But for us there remains a spark of friendship, and we wait together in the quiet for a while. Then I say goodbye with a hug and a kiss (words are almost useless), and, on my way, dutifully stop to greet her roommate.

The roommate is a tiny, aged woman and she wants to talk. She boasts that she will soon be a hundred years old. I believe her. Before her next birthday, she says, she expects to be "flapping angels' wings"! Her deeply creased face is dark, a strong face against the white sheets, stretching up to her neck: almost an angel already. Her body is still and her dark eyes flash. She was raised an orphan and passed from one family to another. Now she has no one, she says, but she's made it through. Am I a doctor? No, I say, a minister. Oh, that's something higher, she says; and she asks me to pray for her, although I feel as if I'm the one who should be asking.

I do, a little awkwardly, and then go. Waiting for the elevator I look at the newly born infants through the window. A nurse smiles, taking me for a father. The babies are naked, and even tinier than my near-centenarian acquaintance; they lie as peacefully as she. I don't know what it all means, ultimately—only that for now it means being with some others for a while, waiting with them and straining to hear what they hear, and to see what they see.

Nature's delicate beauty, friendships confirmed with love, new friends found in unexpected places, words of great courage, quiet waiting, a newborn infant, our own unaccountable joy: such are the signals of transcendence that come to us, that lift us up and put us down again, gently, in a new place.

Be attentive to them, tell your story about them, and be faithful to the messages they bear.

Notes

Introduction

1. Jacob Trapp, *Dawn to Dusk Meditations* (privately published, Santa Fe, NM, 1986), p. 63.

2. See Bernard Lonergan, *Method in Theology* (New York: Herder and Herder, 1972), pp. 13–15. Lonergan thinks this pattern of mental operations is invariant, regardless of subject matter or culture. We need not validate this claim, I believe, to see that the pattern he proposes is a powerful heuristic device.

3. The phrase is from Nathan Söderblom, the liberal Swedish Lutheran theologian and Archbishop of Uppsala in the early twentieth century. James Luther Adams once cited his remark that "Bach's *St. Matthew Passion* should be called the Fifth Evangelist."

4. Many religious people think that theology is dispensable "intellectualizing," but the result often reduces religion to presumptuous moralizing. In

his forthcoming autobiography, *Not Without Dust and Heat*, the late James Luther Adams recites the following story, as told with great enjoyment by Rudolf Otto, the German theologian best known for his book, *The Idea of the Holy* (1923). Otto recalled a prolix American preacher speaking at an international conference. When he had spoken a long paragraph and paused for the translation, the interpreter said, "The speaker has spoken with great eloquence, and has declared that it is good to be good." The man proceeded and, at his second pause, the interpreter said, "The speaker has again spoken eloquently, and declared that it is *indeed* good to be good." The man again proceeded to speak at length; at his third pause the interpreter said, "The speaker has declared, with great eloquence, that indeed, it is *very good* to be good."

5. The poem, no. 822, has two more stanzas. See *The Poems of Emily Dickinson*, edited by Thomas H. Johnson (Cambridge, MA: Harvard University Press, 1958), Vol. II, pp. 622–623.

6. James Luther Adams, *The Prophethood of All Believers*, edited and with an introduction by George K. Beach (Boston: Beacon Press, 1986), pp. 22, 178.

7. On the history and varieties of existentialism, see "The Existential Thesis," James Luther Adams, *An Examined Faith* (Boston: Beacon Press, 1991), pp. 172–185.

8. "For every question for intelligence, there is a corresponding question for reflection; and all questions for reflection have the peculiarity that they can be answered appropriately simply by saying 'Yes' or 'No.' If I ask what a body is, I can also ask whether there are bodies." Bernard Lonergan, *Insight: A Study of Human Understanding* (London: Darton, Longman and Todd Ltd., 1957), pp. 82–83. In other words, to ask what something is, is to ask about its intelligible meaning; to ask whether it exists, the "existential question," is to ask for a reflective judgment. The basic distinction here is between meaning and judgment, or between understanding and decision. Thus, if the answer is yes or no, the question has elicited not a description but an affirmation or a denial. The religious quest includes questions of intellectual meaning and validity, but moves in the existential direction, toward questions of decision and commitment. It engages the heart and the will.

1. The Heart's Directive

1. Denise Levertov,"The Fountain," in *Poems, 1960-1967* (New York: New Directions, 1983), p. 55.

2. Transcript, National Public Radio/*All Things Considered*, December 10, 1991 (Washington, DC).

3. Quoted by Douglas H. Olson, "Such Stuff as Dreams:

The Poetry of Howard Nemerov," *Imagination and Spirit*, edited by Charles Huttar (Grand Rapids, MI: Erdmann's, 1971), pp. 365ff. Nemerov, a former Poet Laureate of the United States, also wrote: "Poetry and institutional religion are in a sense the flowing and static forms of the same substance, liquid and solid states of the same elementary energy. . . . So the work of art is religious in nature, not because it beautifies an ugly world or pretends that a naughty world is a nice one—for these things especially art does not do—but because it shows of its own nature that things drawn within the sacred circle of its forms are transfigured, illumined by an inward radiance which amounts to goodness because it amounts to being itself."

4. For the complete text of "Directive," see *Complete Poems of Robert Frost* (New York: Holt, Reinhart, and Winston, 1949), p. 520. Frost's imagery of the source of spiritual renewal—cold, flowing water—is notably similar to Denise Levertov's, in the poem cited at the beginning of the chapter.

5. James Luther Adams, *The Prophethood of All Believers*, edited and with an introduction by George K. Beach (Boston: Beacon Press, 1986), pp. 22, 178.

6. Richard R. Niebuhr, "The Tragic Play of Symbols," *Harvard Theological Review*, 1982, 75 : 1, pp. 25–33.

7. I use quotation marks here because Klee is using

"the animals" and "the gods" symbolically. Literal animals—my dog, for instance—certainly have feelings and instincts that are akin to thoughts. Similarly, "the gods" spoken of literally, could only be God. The question of whether God suffers, enjoys, or experiences other human-like emotions is a theological conundrum, but God as presented in the Bible certainly does. Thus, taken literally, Klee's parable—like any parable or metaphor— would be misunderstood. Kenneth Burke lays great stress on this point: to take a metaphor literally (without mentally "discounting" it) is to misunderstand it. In fact, as Burke argues in *The Rhetoric of Religion* (Boston: Beacon Press, 1961) pp. 17ff, the capacity to use language depends on one's capacity to distinguish between a word and the thing it symbolizes by "discounting" (partially negating).

2. Naming God

1. Sharon D. Welch, *A Feminist Ethic of Risk* (Minneapolis: Fortress Press, 1990), pp. 178–79.

2. Since names (as concepts or ideas) are composed of letters (characters), Plato used "letter" as a metaphor of the parts into which concepts can be broken (analysis), and recombined again into wholes (synthesis). Following Plato's lead, Erich Frank writes: "The word 'letter' can be regarded as a symbol for

any universal concept, gained through logical analysis, ... the opposite of original unity, of the 'spirit,' which gives the letter its proper meaning." See Erich Frank, *Philosophical Understanding and Religious Truth* (London: Oxford University Press, 1945), p. 165.

Bach's transposition of his name into musical notation is based on German musical convention, in which "B" equals B-flat and "H" equals B; thus Bach's name is musically read:

B-flat, A, C, B. For discussion of Bach's use of his name in "The Art of the Fugue," see Donald R. Hofstadter, *Gödel, Escher, Bach: An Eternal Golden Braid* (New York: Vintage Books, 1980), pp. 79–81, 86.

3. *Measure for Measure*, Act 1, Scene 1, lines 27–30. That Shakespeare thinks of Angelo as archetypal man is suggested by Psalm 8, "Thou hast made him [the human being] a little lower than the angels," and by the sacred allegory that underlies the play: the Duke is God in absentia, leaving this "Angelo" to rule on earth in his stead. Whether this rule will be for good or for ill remains to be seen, in his "history."

4. To be sure, Emily Dickinson imagined ecclesiastical insects ("It was a short procession,—/The bobolink was there,/An aged bee addressed us,/And then we knelt in prayer."—lines from "The Gentian

Weaves Her Fringes"), but the idea of the proud Olympians of ancient Greece going to church is comic. Fables, of course, are works of the imagination in which the real subject is human life. The parable of Paul Klee alluded to here is recited in Chapter 1.

5. William Shakespeare, *Macbeth*, Act V, Scene 5, lines 24–28.

6. Bernard Lonergan writes: "The possibility of inquiry on the side of the subject lies in his intelligence, in his drive to know what, why, how, and in this ability to reach intellectually satisfying answers. But why should the answers that satisfy the intelligence of the subject yield anything more than a subjective satisfaction? Why should they be supposed to possess any relevance to knowledge of the universe? Of course, we assume that they do. We can point to the fact that our assumption is confirmed by its fruits. So implicitly we grant that the universe is intelligible and, once that is granted, there arises the question whether the universe could be intelligible without having an intelligent ground. But that is the question about God." *Method in Theology* (New York: Herder and Herder, 1972), p. 101.

7. James Luther Adams, *An Examined Faith*, edited and with an introduction by George K. Beach (Boston: Beacon Press, 1991), p. 20.

8. Adams, *An Examined Faith*, p. 361.

9. I think people know this intuitively. A purely abstract, impersonal God may be intellectually interesting but finally invites its own rejection as an object of religious devotion. Paul Tillich pointed out that "person" is not a biological but a moral category. Although I wouldn't go so far as to call my dog a person, my relationship to him is personal insofar as it is qualified by a moral regard not utterly different from what I accord human beings. Can I rise to an equally personal regard for or in relationship to God?

10. We become human persons in relationship—to parents, friends, comrades, compatriots, lovers, spouses, etc. But the relationship is dialectical; that is, it includes opposition and tension as well as likeness and harmony, differentiation as well as identity. Classical theology has affirmed of the human being both an original likeness to God and an ultimate difference from God, two assertions that can only be united dialectically. They may, however, be narratively linked, as in the Genesis story of the Creation and Fall—being made in the image of God and willfully violating God's original intent. The narrative sequence parallels the child's gradual movement from identity with his or her parents to differentiation from them; an intermediate stage of conflict is a psychodynamic necessity.

11. Albert Camus once said—as I recall the statement—
that no one can tell himself who he is, or herself who
she is, but we depend on someone else to tell us. I
agree, and yet how oppressive it would be to be
wholly defined by others! This two-fold reflection
leads to the idea that only a personal relation to
ultimate being, that is, to God, liberates us to
achieve fuller self-knowledge. Thus, we seek a
transcendent Other, that is, a God who "defines" us
as centers of creative freedom. On the latter concept, see Chapter 4.

12. "Press it": God (that which is truly sacred) cannot
be depersonalized because God cannot be objecti-
fied—made into an "it," a finite thing or idea. The
same hedge against idolatry underlies Jesus' radical admonition, "Swear not . . . but let your word
be 'Yes' or 'No'" (Matthew 5 : 34-37); the reason is
that swearing "in the name of God" implies binding
God to our purposes. Many profound thinkers have
insisted upon the *via negativa* as the only way to
God, for instance Simone Weil: "To believe in God
is not a decision we can make. All we can do is to
decide not to give our love to false gods." She means,
I believe, that we cannot appropriate God
to ourselves, but can only allow ourselves to be
appropriated by God through a radical dispossession of self.

3. The Human Condition

1. Howard Nemerov, "On Going Down in History,"
   The Christian Century, November 27, 1968.

2. W. H. Auden, "For the Time Being," in *Religious
   Drama I* (New York: Living Age Books, 1957), p. 30.
   The Joseph referred to here is the husband of Mary,
   who in faith chooses her again despite the doubt
   surrounding Jesus' paternity and his (poetically
   imagined) shame.

3. "Self-appropriation" is Bernard Lonergan's shorthand expression for a basic aim of his "transcendental method," an analysis of "the conscious and
   intentional operations" of the mind. By "appropri-
   ating" our central intellectual and moral capacities
   (observing attentively, understanding intelligently, deciding reasonably, acting responsibly) we are
   able to overcome biases and advance in thought in
   order to achieve self-transcendence. See Lonergan,
   Method in Theology, pp. 13–16, 268.

4. One way of "thinking out loud" would be to follow
   René Descartes's method: "I should be glad . . . in
   this discourse to describe for the benefit of others
   the paths I have followed, to paint a picture, as it
   were, of my life, of which each one may judge as he
   pleases; and I should be happy, too, to learn what
   public opinion has to say of me, and so discover a
   fresh mode of instruction of myself, which I shall

add to those I am already accustomed to employ."
Discourse on Method and Other Writings, trans-
lated with an introduction by Arthur Wollaston
(Baltimore: Penguin Books, 1960), pp. 37–38.

5. William Shakespeare, *Hamlet*, Act III, Scene 1, line
56.

6. Church historian Sidney E. Mead has called the
United States "the nation with the soul of a church."
See his book by the same title (New York: Harper
and Row, 1975), pp. 48–77. Lincoln may have so
closely identified his personal fate with that of the
nation—and encouraged people to so identify him—
that he intentionally avoided identifying with a
particular religious body. In a letter he once said he
would join the church that put only the Great
Commandment of Jesus over its entranceway, the
words which I freely translate, "You shall love God
with all you've got and your neighbor at least as
much as you love yourself, if not more." But see
Matthew 22 : 37ff for a more precise rendering.

7. Reinhold Niebuhr, writing on "the superior depth
and purity" of Lincoln's religious convictions, accents his sensitivity to "the relation of our moral
commitments in history to our religious reservations about the partiality of our moral judgments." Niebuhr cites Lincoln's moral judgment
on slavery: "It may seem strange that any men

should dare to ask a just God's assistance in wringing their bread from the sweat of other men's faces," followed by his religious reservation (recalling the words of Jesus): "But let us judge not, that we be not judged." He concludes: "The prayers of both could not be answered—that of neither have been fully answered." This suggests that history (under divine providence?) will render the final judgment. From this Niebuhr draws a characteristically Niebuhrian conclusion: "It was Lincoln's achievement to embrace a paradox which lies at the center of the spirituality of all Western culture: affirmation of a meaningful history along with religious reservation about the partiality and bias which human actors and agents betray in their definition of that meaning." See Reinhold Niebuhr, "The Religion of Abraham Lincoln," *The Christian Century*, February 10, 1965, p. 173.

8. Hannah Arendt, *The Human Condition* (Garden City, NY: Doubleday Anchor Books, 1959), pp. 12–13. Arendt's thought is characteristic of the "existential turn" in modern thought; her focus is on humanity as subjected to, rather than abstracted from, the limiting conditions of human existence.

9. This insight of the German philosopher Friedrich Schelling is the basis of his criticism of Hegel's idealistic dialectic: There is no smooth, logical movement from thesis to antithesis to synthesis; a

creative leap of the imagination or an act of will—
something logically unaccountable—must enter
the picture. Hence Schelling's "existential dialectic," an idea that influenced Kierkegaard, Marx,
and, in our century, Paul Tillich. On Schelling's role
in the origins of existentialism, see James Luther
Adams, *An Examined Faith*, p. 178.

10. See Matthew 5 : 8. Jesus' words on "counting the
cost" before you undertake a building or a battle
convey the same point: only total commitment will
carry the day (see Luke 14 : 28–32).

11. Irving Kristol is an influential conservative social
and political writer. Before dismissing his quip as a
cheap shot, liberals (among whom I count myself)
should consider that they often seem to use sociological or other "explanations" of violent crime as
exemptions from personal moral responsibility. A
communitarian ethic accents the interdependence
of person and society. Its vision is "covenantal":
the individual must be held accountable to the
moral covenant of society, and at the same time, the
society must be committed to mending its "broken
covenant," that is, its systemic social injustices.
See George K. Beach, "Tolstoy's Question: By What
Right Do Some Persons Punish Other Persons?" in
The Best of Kairos (Boston: Skinner House Books,
1982), pp. 121–32.

12. Lest we make an idol of "freedom," we should recognize the Nazi abuse of *Freiheit*. See Joseph Fisher's story of his encounter with young Nazis before the Second World War, in *Living Religion*, by Joseph L. Fisher and Margaret W. Fisher (Arlington, VA: Clerestory Press, 1993), p. 208.

13. I wince at simplistic statements about "the defeat" of Communism, described as an "evil empire" that sought only global enslavement. Demonizing Communism obscures the fact that it was genuinely utopian. Its idealistic ends were tragically distorted by totalitarian means. Capitalist utopianism, the belief that "market forces" will solve all our social problems and usher in a millennium of peace and prosperity, is our new grand illusion. Mindlessly followed, it too has tragic consequences.

4. Creative Freedom

1. A chief characteristic of religious liberalism is the linkage of religious faith and social-ethical commitment; cut that nerve and it dies. Channing, the chief inspirer of Unitarianism in America, addresses precisely this connection in the passage that follows the foregoing citation: "Christianity has taught me to respect my race, and to reprobate its oppressors. It is because I have learned to regard man

under the light of this religion, that I cannot bear to see him treated as a brute, insulted, wronged, enslaved, made to wear a yoke, to tremble before his brother, to serve him as a tool, to hold property and life at his will, to surrender intellect and conscience to the priest, or to seal his lips or belie his thoughts through dread of the civil power. . . . It is because the human being has moral powers, because he carries a law in his own breast, and was made to govern himself, that I cannot endure to see him taken out of his own hands and fashioned into a tool by another's avarice or pride. It is because I see in him a great nature, the divine image, and vast capacities, that I demand for him means of self-development, spheres for free action; that I call society not to fetter, but to aid his growth." *The Works of William E. Channing, D.D.* (Boston: American Unitarian Association, 1895), pp. 6–8. For Channing's development of the idea of spiritual freedom, see his Election Day Sermon (1830), in this volume.

2. Viktor Frankl, *Man's Search for Meaning*—originally titled *From Death Camp to Existentialism* (Boston: Beacon Press, 1960); see pp. 58ff.

3. See Exodus 3 : 4. The stories of Moses, although they come earlier in the Biblical text, reflect the conception of prophetic vocation developed in Israel centuries later. For the classic stories of the

prophets' "calls," see Jeremiah 1 and Isaiah 6.

4. In *An Open Letter to the Christian Nobility of the German Nation* (1520) Luther wrote: "We must put a bit in the mouth of the Fuggers and similar corporations. How is it possible that in the lifetime of a single man such great possessions, worthy of a king, can be piled up, and yet everything be done legally and according to God's will? I am not a mathematician, but I do not understand how a man with a hundred gulden can make a profit of twenty gulden in one year, nay, how with one gulden he can make another; and that, too, by another way than agriculture or cattle-raising, in which increase of wealth depends not on human wits, but on God's blessing." Martin Luther, *Three Treatises* (Philadelphia: The Muhlenberg Press, 1943), pp. 107–108.

5. See James Luther Adams, *The Prophethood of All Believers*, edited and with an introduction by George K. Beach (Boston: Beacon Press, 1986), p. 7. Adams frequently uses the idea of vocation, in various contexts, in this and other books.

6. The social philosopher Hannah Arendt distinguished "the private realm," including labor and the household, and "the public realm," including politics and social institutions. She was alarmed by what she described as the withering of the public realm in the modern world—the loss of a sense of "public space"

in which all citizens have active roles. See *The Human Condition* (New York: Doubleday Anchor Books, 1958), pp. 45ff. Symptomatic of the loss lamented by Arendt is the way many politicians pander to popular cynicism about "politicians" and the political process itself. Ironically, they run for public office by "running against the government."

7. This view is held by the feminist Old Testament scholar Phyllis Trible. Her interpretation of the creation story in Genesis 1 and 2 is summarized by Cullen Murphy (*Atlantic Monthly*, August, 1993, p. 50): ". . . It is a mistake, in Trible's view, to think of the first human being, Adam, as male. She points out that the Hebrew word *'adham*, from which 'Adam' derives, is a generic term for humankind—it denotes a being created from the earth—and is used to describe a creature of undifferentiated sex. Only when [Yahweh] takes a rib from *'adham* to make a companion are the sexes differentiated, and the change is signaled by a change in terminology. The creature from whom the rib was taken is referred to not as *'adham* but as *'ish* ('man'), and the creature fashioned from the rib is called *'ish-shah* ('woman'). In Trible's reading, the sexes begin in equality." For her full discussion of these questions, see Phyllis Trible, *God and the Rhetoric of Sexuality* (Philadelphia, PA: Fortress Press, 1978), pp. 15–21. This section concludes with a paragraph

that makes an important theological point: The differentiation of the sexes into male and female (or indeed, sexuality itself) is both a positive clue to "the image of God" and, at the same time, a safeguard against an idolatrous identification of God with any one image.

In regard to Yahweh's male identity in the biblical text, it may be noted that the Old Testament is remarkably "unmythic" in the sense that it is very reticent about the nature of God or any other supernatural beings, such as angels, demons, or Satan. Thus Yahweh, although male, has no female consort, in heaven or on earth. He does not create by sexual generation but, like an oriental despot, by saying "Let there be . . . ," that is, by sovereign will. As a result, biblical monotheism lends itself to its own demythologizing: literal readings of its stories are misreadings. Stories of the gods (myths) are meaningful, serious, and sometimes funny, but they are not to be taken utterly seriously, that is, literally. W. H. Auden defined idolatry as taking what is frivolous seriously.

8. The underlying philosophical argument, here, is between idealism and realism—between a "sentimental idealism" that imagines we can return to "a state of nature" and a "critical realism" that knows we cannot and accepts moral responsibility for the fact. It should be noted that secularization, by

canceling the sacred context of our natural and social existence, gives "realism" its value-disregarding connotation. In brief, Genesis will never make sense if the God who creates by sovereign good will is jettisoned from the poem; we will simply say things like, "we humans make 'God' in *our* image," and think it's a wonderful insight.

9. The sense of not just choosing but of being chosen—or of not just pursuing our own purposes, but of being sent on a mission—may *seem* arrogant, but it is precisely the position of anyone democratically elected to an office. It becomes arrogant when it is not understood as a being called to serve, or "a walking *humbly* with thy God" (Micah 6 : 8). Here again, secularization makes nonsense out of ideas that are valid only in a sacred context. The Hebrew prophets turned their people's "chosenness" into burden of moral responsibility. Amos said it devastatingly in a few words: "Thus saith the Lord: Only you have I known of all the peoples of the earth; therefore I will punish you for all your iniquities." (Amos 3 : 2)

10. Dag Hammarskjold, *Markings* (New York: Alfred A. Knopf, 1970), p. 205.

5. The Moral Covenant

1. James Luther Adams, *The Prophethood of All Be-*

lievers, edited and with an introduction by George
K. Beach (Boston: Beacon Press, 1986), pp. 137–138.

2. Hannah Arendt, *The Human Condition* (Garden
City, NY: Doubleday Anchor Books, 1959), pp. 212–
213.

3. It is common sense to recognize that judgments of
what we "ought" to do are rooted in a vision or
general idea of reality, what ultimately "is" the
case. I am aware that this is precisely what I was
taught in college philosophy courses *not* to do.
Indeed, it seems to violate Aristotle's law of the
excluded middle—something cannot be A and not-
A at the same time. However, dialectic is a logic
that deals with internal contradictions: what is
untrue at one level may be true at another. The
moral covenant *describes* at one level and *pre-
scribes* at the other. On the priority of "isness" over
"oughtness," see James Luther Adams's comments
on the thought of Friedrich von Hügel, in *The
Prophethood of All Believers*, pp. 62–64.

4. Transcript, *All Things Considered*, National Public
Radio, December 10, 1991 (Washington, DC).

5. At least two moral concerns arise here: the alleged
rape and the tactics of prosecution. A third concern
is the handling of this item by the media. A parent
said to me that the program's explicit language
about sexual functions intruded on her young

daughter's privacy. I agreed with the parent. National Public Radio later commented on this kind of concern and modified its policy on reporting sexual matters to be more circumspect.

6. See Joseph Fletcher, *Situation Ethics: The New Morality* (Philadelphia: The Westminster Press, 1964).

7. I have developed this theme more fully in an essay, "Covenantal Ethics," in *A Life of Choice: Some Liberal Religious Perspectives on Morality*, edited by Clark Kucheman (Boston: Beacon Press, 1977), pp. 107–125.

8. On "the covenant of being," see James Luther Adams, *The Prophethood of All Believers*, pp. 137, 248.

9. These four questions run parallel to the first four chapters of this book. They deal, respectively, with religious awareness ("The Heart's Directive"), understanding ("Naming God"), valuing ("The Human Condition"), and commitment ("Creative Freedom"). "The Moral Covenant," then, marks the central turning point in this study: it fulfills our "creative freedom" at the level of commitment and action; it also sets the stage for the problem of spiritual transformation ("newmindedness") at the level of judgment and decision, which follows it. For further comments on these structural issues,

see the Introduction.

10. The founding charter of Judaism is the covenant between God and Israel, initiated by Moses and encapsuled in "the ten words" (the Commandments). The Book of Joshua, Chapter 24, gives an idealized account of a "covenant renewal ceremony."

11. See especially Alasdair MacIntyre, *After Virtue: A Study in Moral Theory*, second edition, (Notre Dame, Indiana: University of Notre Dame Press, 1984).

12. On the life and thought of Dr. Fisher, see *Living Religion*, by Joseph L. Fisher and Margaret W. Fisher, edited and with an introduction by George Kimmich Beach and Barbara Kres Beach (Arlington, VA: Clerestory Press, 1993).

13. The symmetry of moral concepts here suggested as the basis of a stable ethical system is similar to Hannah Arendt's comments on the symmetry between "forgiving" and "promising," in the passage cited at the beginning of the chapter. Another example of "moral symmetry" is reflected in the conclusion to Carol Gilligan's influential book on the differences between the moral sensibilities of women and men (focusing, respectively, on "care" and on "fairness"):

"To understand how the tension between responsibilities and rights sustains the dialectic of human development is to see the integrity of two disparate modes of experience that are in the end connected. While an ethic of justice proceeds from the premise of equality . . . an ethic of care rests on the premise of nonviolence. . . . In the representation of maturity, both perspectives converge in the realization that just as inequality adversely affects both parties in an unequal relationship, so too violence is destructive for everyone involved. This dialogue between fairness and care not only provides a better understanding of relations between the sexes but also gives rise to a more comprehensive portrayal of adult work and family relationships." *In a Different Voice: Psychological Theory and Women's Development* (Cambridge, MA: Harvard University Press, 1982), p. 174.

6. Newmindedness

1. Howard Thurman, *The Growing Edge* (Richmond, IN: Friends United Press, 1956), p. 34.

2. Compulsive negativism, or skepticism that serves no purpose, is without redeeming spiritual value. However, a healthy skepticism is a tool of truth-telling, in the face of excessive credulity. (The human mind, said John Calvin, is an eternal factory of idols.) Skepticism is needed, then, in service of religious authenticity. Anyone who has read the

prophets of ancient Israel knows that religion, *per se*, is not good: "I hate your feast days . . . ," Amos thundered. Jesus likewise excoriated public displays of piety. In *Murder in the Cathedral*, T. S. Eliot wrote: "The last temptation is the greatest treason / To do the right thing for the wrong reason."

3. Dietrich Bonhoeffer, *Letters and Papers from Prison* (London and Glasgow: S.C.M. Press, 1953), p. 83.

4. Public prayer, like all things performed before an audience, is an art form; that does not make it any less authentic than spontaneous prayer, just as written music is neither more nor less authentic than improvised music. However, an overly refined or formal prayer seems insincere, not "from the heart." Paul's words, "Likewise the Spirit helps us in our weakness; for we do not know how to pray as we ought, but the Spirit himself intercedes for us with sighs too deep for words" (Romans 8 : 26), suggest that a prayer may be incompetent, but the divine Spirit can transform it into something better. In other words, an authentic prayer does not depend on the technique, refinement, or tradition, or on the status of the one who prays. There is always something inarticulate—a "sigh too deep for words"—in a true prayer, and just this is the Spirit at work in us.

5. The final touchstone of authentic prayer is self-

abandonment or surrender to the will of God. The classic example, reflecting both "surrender" and the entirely human wish to be spared the suffering it will bring, is Jesus' prayer in the Garden of Gethsemane: "And he went a little farther and fell on his face, and prayed, saying, O my Father, if it be possible, let this cup pass from me: nevertheless not as I will but as thou wilt." (Matthew 26 : 39; King James Version) Albrecht Dürer depicted Jesus' "Agony in the Garden" several times in various media. His 1521 drawing of the scene, with Jesus prone on the ground but seeming to float in the air, is incomparably moving. It is reproduced in Erwin Panofsky's *Albrecht Dürer* (Princeton: Princeton University Press, 1945), Vol. 2, fig. 273.

6. We imagine that "faith" was easier in an earlier, "credulous" age. That this is not so—not, at least, at the existential level—is suggested by the story of a father's struggle with faith in Mark 9 : 14–29. See my interpretation of this passage in "Christian Humanism," *Unitarian Universalism 1986: Selected Essays* (Boston: Unitarian Universalist Ministers Association, 1986), p. 101.

7. Reinhold Niebuhr, *Essays in Applied Christianity* (New York: Living Age Books, 1959), p. 30.

8. James Luther Adams cites Cadbury's words in *The Prophethood of All Believers*, p. 172.

9. The term "newminded" was first suggested to me by Richard R. Niebuhr: "The little word faith stands as a shorthand sign . . . for the ever new mindfulness that one is shaped by God-ruling." (Niebuhr also says: "God-ruling is a phrase intended to underscore the dynamism and action character of *basileia tou theou*"—the Greek phrase usually translated "kingdom of God.") See "Religion Within Limits," *Harvard Divinity School Bulletin* , 1968, New Series. Vol. 1, No. 2: 2, 6.

10. "I came not to abolish but to fulfill the law" (Matthew 5 : 17). *Metanoia* or "newmindedness" is a matter of decision, the transformation and renewal of the will. Without radical renewal, moral covenants (discussed in the preceding chapter) degenerate into contracts, bargains, or even "pacts with the devil." Accordingly, forgiveness does not abolish but fulfills the moral covenant; it enables its fulfillment by releasing us from its demands, strictly or legalistically interpreted, for the sake of a new beginning. "Newmindedness" precedes "the dedicated community" (discussed in the following chapter) because it nourishes the community that is dedicated to sustaining these understandings.

7. The Dedicated Community

1 . The Rev. Johnny Ray Youngblood is addressing the

staff of his congregation, St. Paul Community Baptist Church in Brooklyn, New York. The words are cited in Samuel G. Freedman's *Upon This Rock: The Miracles of a Black Church* (New York: Harper Collins, 1993), pp. 34-35.

2. Cited by F. Forrester Church, *The Devil and Dr. Church* (San Francisco: Harper and Row, 1986), p. x. Chesterton also said that angels can fly because "they take themselves lightly." If Satan is a fallen angel, one sees that the difference between good and evil is that evil is not a positive power in its own right, but a distortion of the good.

3. *Measure for Measure*, Act 2, Scene 2, lines 120ff.

4. The unhappy consequences of American individualism are described by Robert Bellah, *et al.* in *Habits of the Heart: Individualism and Commitment in American Life* (Berkeley and Los Angeles: University of California Press, 1985).

5. See John A. Buehrens and F. Forrester Church, *Our Chosen Faith* (Boston: Beacon Press, 1989), p. 5.

6. Paul Weiss, *The God We Seek* (Carbondale, IL: Southern Illinois University Press, 1964); see pp. 99–103. Weiss writes: "Ideally, the dedicated community has a plurality of functions. It edifies, disciplines, supports and protects its members. It therefore insists on calling their attention to the primary

facts on which it is grounded. . . . Historic occasions are commemorated in its holidays, ceremonials, and references, to make it the locus of an accumulation of traditions and funded knowledge. It is the ground for a determinate expectation with respect to the future of the group, and a defining base for an ideal end. A training ground, a laboratory, an educational centre, the dedicated community enables men to find their proper place in relation to God. . . . [It] offers a sanctuary set off over against the rest of the world in which men can find some indication as to how they ought to direct their energies and use their time."

7. The universal meaning of the story is that every people constitutes itself through acts of self-determination, and every people has this right. (The American Declaration of Independence illustrates both assertions.) It is important to emphasize the universality of this principle in the face of the refusal by Jewish fundamentalists to recognize the right of the Palestinian people to self-determination. This "right," it should be noted, cannot be maintained in the abstract but must be actively claimed by the group in question, as the Palestinians and others have done in the contemporary world. In other words, "rights" seem to be historically relative. The Christian story universalizes and personalizes the theme; however, a regression

to particularism—no salvation outside the Church" and "there is only one true Church"—similarly mars Christian history. And yet there is another side to this picture, too: "universalism," which cancels all particular historical memories, making everything equal with the wave of a wand and conflating the sacred and the profane, tends to be self-liquidating. Every group must define its boundaries and celebrate its particular story, or it is kaput.

8. An account of this art education program, using Barbara Beach's dance work in the museum as a chief illustration, is found in *Object Lessons: Cleveland Creates a Museum*, edited by Evan H. Turner (Cleveland: The Cleveland Museum of Art, 1991), p. 164.

9. William Shakespeare, *Hamlet*, Act 2, Scene 2, lines 590–591.

10. James Luther Adams, *The Prophethood of All Believers*, pp. 36–37. Bach's *St. Matthew Passion* and *St. John Passion* are based on the texts of "The Passion Story," the last days of Jesus' life, from Matthew 26–27 and John 18–19.

11. See my essay, "Christian Humanism," in *Unitarian Universalism 1986: Selected Essays* (Boston: Unitarian Universalist Ministers Association, 1986), pp. 93–108.

8. Parabolic Vision

1. Dag Hammarskjold, *Markings*, translated by Leif Sjoberg and W. H. Auden (New York: Alfred A. Knopf, 1970), p. 71.

2. Howard Nemerov, "Runes" (lines 1–6), *New and Selected Poems* (Chicago: The University of Chicago Press [Phoenix Books], 1960), p. 4.

3. Quoted by James Luther Adams, *An Examined Faith*, p. 329.

4. Cited by W. H. Auden, *A Certain World: A Commonplace Book* (New York: The Viking Press, 1970), under the heading of "Prayer."

5. Paul's words are often cited as if they required belief in the physical resurrection of Jesus: "If Christ has not been raised, your faith is futile and you are still in your sins" (I Corinthians 15 : 17). Paul goes on to ask, rhetorically, "How are the dead raised?" and answers that the "physical body" is transformed by the power of God into an immortal "spiritual body." This passage is obscure, and in its conclusion, ecstatic. But clearly for Paul the whole meaning of Jesus' life and death turns on this transformation: the one whom the world rejected, God accepted; whom the world killed, God gave new life. Thus the Resurrection symbolizes a spiritual transformation that conquers the power of death and sin over

life. By identifying with Jesus' resurrection—by faith—we appropriate our own resurrection. Whether or not the reader finds these conceptions meaningful (and certainly they deserve closer examination than I have given here), it can be seen that Paul insists on the resurrection of Jesus because it fulfills the logic of faith. In short, it "makes sense" of Jesus' life and death, and by identification with him, of our own.

6. Dag Hammarskjold, *Markings*, p. 71.

7. See Romans 7 : 7–20. The paradox leads Paul to reflect on the contradictoriness and insufficiency of will: "For I do not do the good that I want, but the evil that I do not want is what I do."

8. Dag Hammarskjold, *Markings*, p. 86. An entry in his journal from several years later (previously cited on page 102), indicates that Hammarskjold believed he did achieve the breakthrough he sought. Several things that reinforce points in this chapter are notable here. (1) The indefinite reference of his words, "I did answer *Yes* to Someone—or Something," reflect an awareness of the symbolic character of expressions of belief. Their content can be given only in reflexive form, as that which enables him to make sense out of an otherwise senseless existence. (2) The entry carries the thought forward in terms of the personal effects (courage and confi-

dence) of his "yes": "From that moment I have known what it means 'not to look back,' and 'to take no thought for the morrow.'" (3) It also answers his poignant longing, from the entry on page 86, to believe that "I am not alone." He continues:

As I continued along the Way, I learned, step by step, word by word, that behind every saying of the Gospels stands *one* man and *one* man's experience. Also behind the prayer that the cup might pass from him and his promise to drink it. Also behind each of the words from the cross.

Hammarskjold is surely wrong to speak of "every saying" as traceable to Jesus. But I agree with his intuitive sense that a sizable number of the sayings—some of them cited in this book—are authentic. I too believe that in the Gospels we are dealing with material that, however overlaid with legend and myth it may be, arose from the incalculably deep impact of a real person.